Comprehensive steps for raising healthy Killifish

Caprii M. Walker

The Ultimate Resource for Creating a Thriving Killifish Aquarium: Essential Tips, Advanced Strategies, and Breathtaking Imagery

Life advices:

Seek mentorship; insights from experienced professionals can be invaluable.

Engage in activities that challenge both mind and body; holistic health is the key to well-being.

Introduction

Welcome to the captivating world of killifish—a diverse and beautiful species of aquarium fish that will capture your imagination and bring vibrant life to your aquatic oasis. Whether you're a seasoned aquarist or a beginner, this comprehensive guide is your gateway to understanding and caring for these fascinating creatures.

In this book, we will embark on an educational journey, unraveling the secrets of killifish and providing you with the knowledge and skills to create a thriving and enchanting killifish aquarium. From the basics of their genus and locality codes to the intricacies of breeding and photography, every aspect of killifish care and enjoyment will be explored.

We begin by introducing you to the world of killifish, offering insights into their diverse genus and the significance of locality codes. Understanding these fundamental aspects will lay the foundation for your exploration of the remarkable species that inhabit this fascinating fish family.

As we delve deeper, we explore the various types of killifish, including annuals, non-annuals, semi-annuals, plant spawners, peat spawners, and peat divers. Discover their unique characteristics and behaviors, and gain a deeper understanding of the different requirements for each type.

To ensure a harmonious and thriving aquarium, we delve into the dynamics of male and female killifish interactions and discuss strategies to manage aggression. With this knowledge, you will be able to select the right combination of killifish for your aquarium, creating a balanced and visually stunning aquatic community.

Creating the perfect habitat for your killifish is essential, and we guide you through the process of setting up an aquarium. From selecting suitable decorations and aqua plants to understanding water quality requirements and conditioning, we equip you with the necessary tools to establish an ideal environment for your fish to thrive.

Step-by-step, we walk you through the process of setting up your killifish aquarium, ensuring that you have a comprehensive understanding of each stage. From routine maintenance to budgeting for your hobby, we cover every aspect of aquarium care, empowering you to become a confident and capable killifish keeper.

As you embark on your killifish journey, we provide valuable insights into buying and keeping killifish. From creating a wish list to ensuring the safe arrival of your fish and matching their water conditions, we guide you through the process of acquiring and acclimating these captivating creatures.

Breeding killifish is a rewarding and fulfilling endeavor, and we explore the techniques and enhancements that will maximize your success. From setup enhancements to semi-automatic water changes and oxygen enhancement, we offer practical advice to optimize your breeding endeavors.

Feeding your killifish is an essential aspect of their care, and we discuss various food options, both purchased and self-cultured. With an understanding of their dietary needs, you will be able to provide a nutritious and balanced diet that promotes their health and vitality.

Lastly, we delve into the art of fish photography, offering tips and techniques to capture the beauty of your killifish. Learn how to showcase their vibrant colors and unique features, preserving their essence in stunning images.

In the pages of this book, you will find a wealth of knowledge, practical advice, and inspiration to embark on a fulfilling journey with killifish. Whether you're a beginner or an experienced aquarist, this guide will empower you to create a captivating and thriving killifish aquarium, filled with life, beauty, and endless fascination. Let us dive into the world of killifish together and unlock the secrets of these mesmerizing creatures.

Contents

Chapter 1: Introduction to Killifish

1.1 Genus

There are several hundred species of killifish. The most popular ones have common names like Blue Gularis, Lyretail, Clown Killifish, and Normani Lampeye. However in situations like buying and selling on the Internet, full scientific names are required to clearly identify a killifish.

Killifish are grouped genetically in genus. You do not have to remember the names of all the genera. All you need to remember is the full names of the killifish that you are keeping or going to buy. To help you memorize, write the names down in a simple text file using a software like Notepad and put this text file on your computer desktop. Text file, unlike Word file or the like, will open up in no time with just a click. Quite simply, the first part of a scientific name designates the genus or sub-genus of the species. For example, the killifish species "Aphanius mento" belongs to the Aphanius genus.

Over the years, not only new species are discovered, some known species were re-classified to another genus   or sub-genus when new scientific evidences support doing so. For example, genera Chromaphyosemion and Diapteron were both regrouped a few years ago to be Aphyosemion. Still, their original genera are being used widely by many killie keepers and breeders.

Do not assume that species of the same genus behave exactly in the same way. Check the Web for species specific information or keeping instructions if you want to know more.

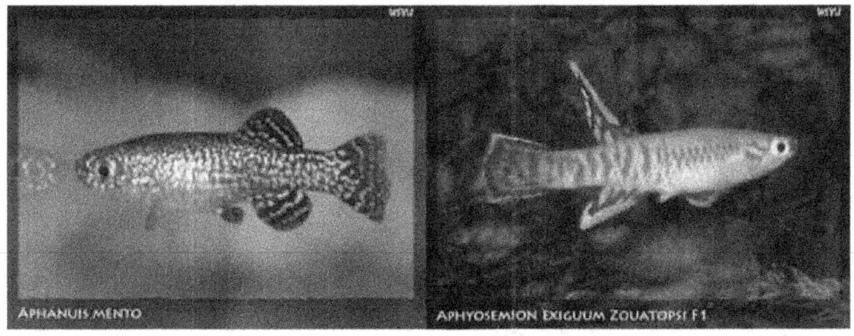

Example of an Aphanius (Left) and Aphyosemion (Right).

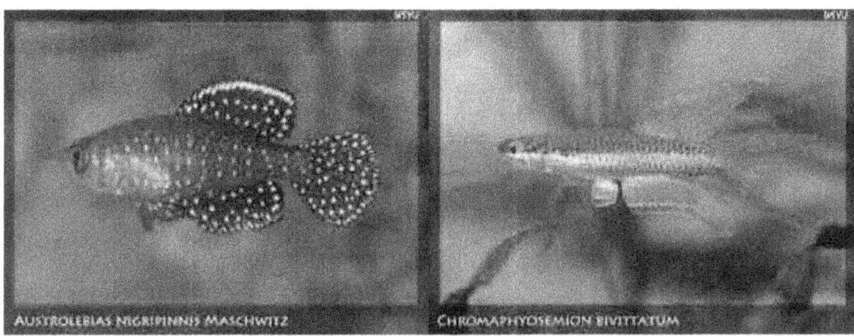

Example of an Austrolebias (Left) and Chromaphyosemion (Right)

Example of a Diapteron (Left) and Epiplatys (Right)

Example of a Fundulopanchax (Left) and Lamprichthys (Right)

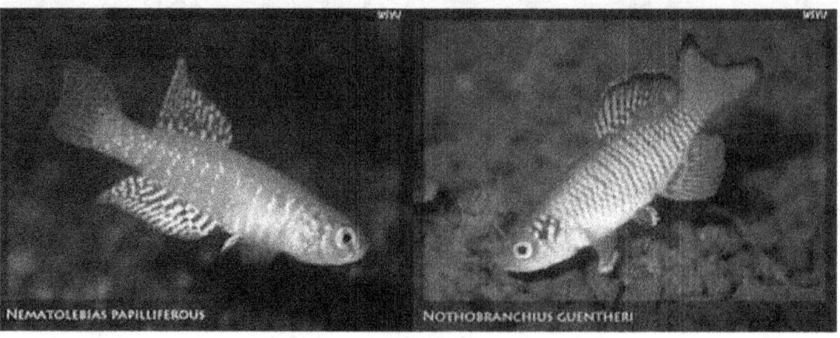

Example of a Nematolebias (Left) and Nothobranchius (Right)

Example of Simpsonichthys, a Pearlfish.

There is one key point to note about killifish species: the killifish keeping community discourages cross breeding species to create species that does not exist in nature. Killie breeders strive to maintain strain purity of the killies that they raise. Nonetheless, accidents did happen and hybrids were discovered. An example of a hybrid, named Aphyosemion austral "Lineatus" by the owner, could be seen at: http://images.killi.net/a/AUS/.

1.2 Locality Code

A collection time and location code would be added to the scientific name of a killifish by the fish collector to better identify the particular species population. For example, the species **Nothobranchius rachovii Nicuadala MOZ 04-10** originated from some Nothobranchius rachovii specimens collected at the 10th registered collection site in Mozambique in 2004. This species is shown in the following photo:

Locality code is sometimes dropped from the name when the species was introduced to the hobby or when the origin is no longer known. When unsure, killie breeders leave the locality code part of the name blank, or label them as AS or Aquarium Strain. e.g. **Nothobranchius rachovii** or **Nothobranchius rachovii AS** is shown below.

And then there may be strains of a species that demonstrate a golden yellow or golden white colour due to natural genetic changes. They are called Albino. e.g. **Nothobranchius rachovii Albino**, as below.

As can be seen above, these 3 strains of Nothobranchius rachovii display different colour forms and patterns.

Finally, you may encounter names of egg or fish ending with F1 or F2. These are not related to the locality code. They are respectively the first and second generation offspring of a wild-catch fish. They are more expensive and more desirable for breeding purposes.

1.3 Three Letter Species Codes

It is good to know that most killifish species are assigned a 3-letter species code. Whenever strain information is not important or relevant, it is suffice to refer to a killifish species by its 3-letter species code. For example, it is fine to write "your BIT looks great" instead of "your Chromaphyosemion bitaeniatum looks great." Codes for some common species are as follows:

Scientific Name	Code	Scientific Name	Code
Aphanius mento	MEN	Lamprichthys tanganicanus	TGN
Aphyosemion australe	AUS	Maratecoara lacortei	LCT
Aphyosemion cognatum	COG	Nothobranchius kafuensis	KAF
Aphyosemion elberti	ELB	Nothobranchius eggersi	EGG
Aphyosemion exiguum	EXO	Nothobranchius foerschi	FOE
Aphyosemion gabunense	GAB	Nothobranchius furzeri	FUR
Chromaphyosemion bitaeniatum	BIT	Nothobranchius guentheri	GUE
Chromaphyosemion alpha	APH	Nothobranchius korthausae	KOR
Diapteron georgiae	GEO	Nothobranchius rachovii	RAC
Fundulopanchax fallax	FAL	Nothobranchius rubripinnis	RUN
Fundulopanchax gardneri	GAR	Simpsonichthys fulminantis	FUM
Fundulopanchax gresensi	GRE	Simpsonichthys magnificus	MAG
Fundulopanchax sjoestedti	SJO	Simpsonichthys picturatus	PCR

1.4 Annuals, Non-Annuals, Semi-Annuals, Plant Spawners, Peat Spawners & Peat Divers

Apart from their genera, killifish are classified according to their general life cycles into three groups: annuals, non-annuals, and semi-annuals.

Annuals - Water in the natural habitats of these seasonal fish like muddy pools and streams dry out in dry seasons. Annuals accommodate by having a lifespan of less than a year. The shortest one being that of the species FUR with a lifespan of about 4 months. Exception is annuals kept in captivity in good conditions. They may live longer than one year.

Annual eggs laid in the muddy bottom develop very slowly and they wait patiently during the rest of the wet season and the dry season that follows. When the first rain comes some weeks or even months later and wets the eggs, the hatching starts. The eggs mature at different speeds so that even if the first rain dries out and kills the newly hatched fry, there will always be more to hatch when the wet season stays.

Depending on the species, average incubation time of annual eggs is from 1 to 6 months. The egg sellers would tell you what time the eggs are collected and what incubation time to use for that particular species. If not, one can easily find such information on the internet. Incubation time is just a reference as storage temperature and moisture could affect the speed of egg development. Killie keeper will start examining the eggs when the incubation time is almost up to make sure that they are in fact well developed before wetting them.

Annual Laying Eggs Over a Bowl of Peat Moss. The species shown is **Nothobranchius guentheri,** or simply **GUE** in short.

Most annuals mate on top of mud or peat moss. The males will bury the eggs after fertilizing them. If only a bare tank or hard substrate like pebbles are provided, they will still lay eggs on hard surfaces. However, the eggs are now exposed to predators and they are also more troublesome to locate and collect.

An Annual Peat Diver is diving into a cup of deep Peat Moss for mating. The species here is **Simpsonichthys fulminantis** or **FUM** in short.

Peat Diver Annuals, on the other hand, bury themselves completely in the mud or peat moss before laying eggs. Peat divers would be confused in an aquarium if they were not given at least a tall cup of peat moss for diving themselves into.

Non-Annual Mating On Plants. The species shown is **Aphyosemion australe Orange**, or **AUS Orange** in short.

Non-Annuals are not seasonal. They live in permanent and not temporary waters. Their lifespan could be as long as a 2-3 years. Such species normally lay eggs everywhere though they prefer to lay eggs on plants. Some species prefer to lay eggs on plants near the surface and some species prefer to lay eggs near the bottom. Eggs of non-annuals develop very quickly in water, if fertilized properly by the male. Incubation time could be as short as 1-2 weeks. Similar to annual eggs, incubation time gets longer if the temperature is cooler or if the eggs are not totally submerged in water. If put on wet peat, incubation time would become longer at 4-6 weeks.

A Semi-Annual with a full name of **Fundulopanchax sjoestedti Dwarf Blue VAKA**. One may just call them **SJO VAKA**.

Midway between annuals and non-annuals are the **Semi-Annuals**. They show characteristics midway between the annuals and non-annuals. They live longer than annuals and their eggs need a longer time to hatch than non-annuals.

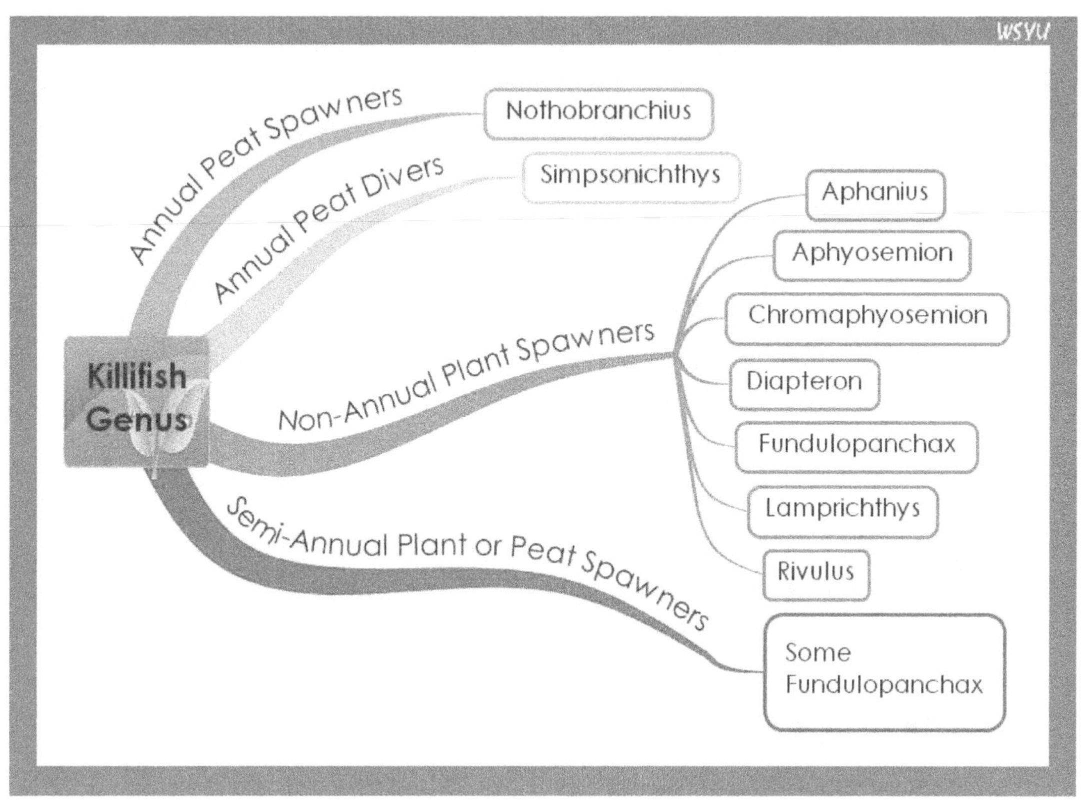

Some Popular Genera Grouped by Lifespan

For egg collections, we use a setup that matches the egg laying habit of each species. We provide a shallow bowl of peat moss or sand to peat spawning annuals, a tall cup of peat moss for peat-diver annuals, floating or sinking mops that mimic plants for non-annuals, and a mixture of both for semi-annuals.

For egg storage and hatching however, it can be very flexible. In general, we can store eggs of any kinds in water   or moist peat moss as long as we understand that temperature and moisture will affect their incubation time. If we are busy and don't have time to take care of them, we keep the eggs cool and moist. If we want to hatch them sooner, we keep them warm and wet. More on that in later chapters.

1.5 Males & Females

Female killifish are in general less colourful than their male counterparts.

Silvery Spotless Females of Nothobranchius. The species here is
Nothobranchius rachovii AS or simply **RAC**.

The females of different Nothobranchius species look very much alike and the males will spawn with all of them. Avoid cross breeding by keeping different Nothobranchius species in different tanks.

A Simpsonichthys fulminantis Couple. They are called **FUM**

Likewise, the females of some Simpsonichthys species look very much alike.

This **FAL** female has rows of dot on the sides.

Male and female do look alike in certain ways! They are **ELB N'tui** by the way.

As in many things, there are exceptions!

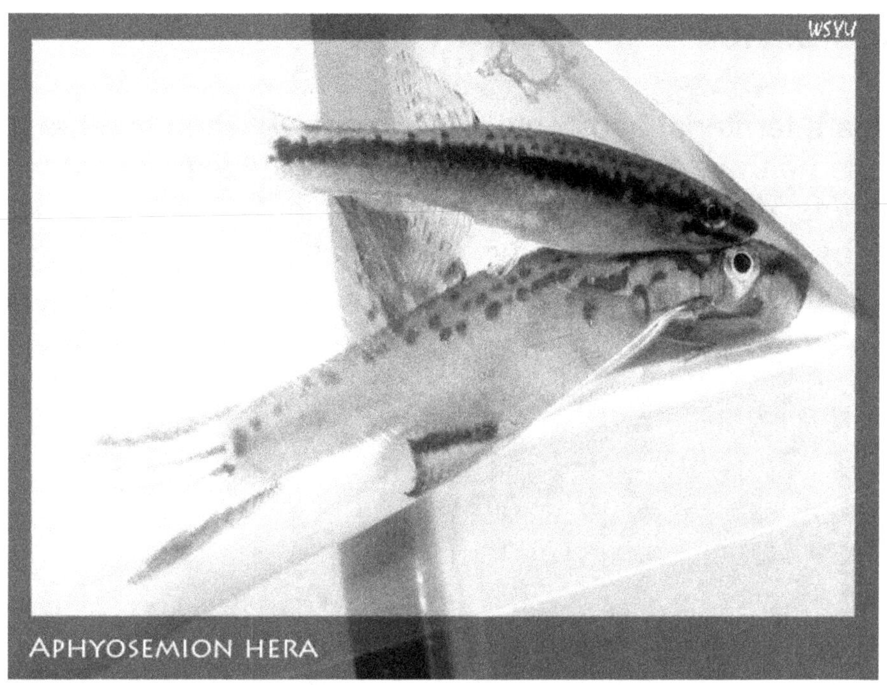

Hera females are more colourful than the males!

1.6 Aggression

Killifish are territorial and could get aggressive when another male or female is nearby. Apart from observing the necessary fish stocking density (as discussed in section 2.5), plants, rocks, woods, etc. should be provided to offer weaker killies space for hiding. Some species are more aggressive than others and beginners may want to avoid the most aggressive kinds.

MAG are relatively easy.

RAC is a bit more aggressive but they don't kill.

MEN is downright deadly.

In the above photo, the **MEN** was about to bite into the FOE. **If not kept in a large group of its own kind**, a MEN will try to kill every other fish in the tank. MEN are also special in that they are highly intelligent. They know how to set another killie up in a chase around well planted objects. In short, MEN kills and they are not for beginners.

1.7 Selecting The Right Killifish For You

Some killifish species are easier to keep than others. These easier killies are much less susceptible to changes in water quality and temperature, less demanding on their food supply and lay a lot of eggs. They are therefore also less expensive. The easiest one of all is **Fundulopanchax gardneri N'sukka** or **GAR N'sukka** as shown below. They lay a lot of eggs every day!

Should beginners buy fish or eggs labelled "for beginners" only? Not really! Just follow the few simple rules that are described in the following chapters and I am sure you will be doing just fine. If you can afford the higher price and do not mind bearing the slightly higher risk of losing those killifish labelled as "not for beginners", just go ahead and buy whichever good looking species that appeal to you most. That's what I did at the beginning any way. If you really want to keep a particular species that looks extra good, you would likely spend more time into their maintenance than a species that you don't particularly like. As a results, a better chance of success!

However, I would still advise beginners to stay away from four species. The first one being Lamprichthys Tanganicanus and other lampeyes. They require extremely stable water conditions. The second one is Aphanius which are too aggressive unless you keep a big group of them. The third one is Diapteron. They need cool water to thrive and a water cooler can be expensive. Many species adapt well to warmer temperature but Diapteron just don't. Finally, avoid Clown killifish or Epiplatys annulatus. They are way too small in size for beginners. Buying fish is discussed in section 3.2 while buying eggs is covered in section 6.1.

End of Chapter One

WSYU
APHYOSEMION CELIAE WINFREDAE

CHROMAPHYOSEMION BITAENIATUM IJEBU ODE

WSYU
APHANUIS MENTO

Chapter 2:   Setting Up An Aquarium

2.1 Layout Possibilities

A well planted big aquarium populated with colourful fish make fish keeping a real relaxing pleasure. (Very nice paintings of killifish by courtesy of Karen Hatzigeorgiou at karenswhimsy.com.)

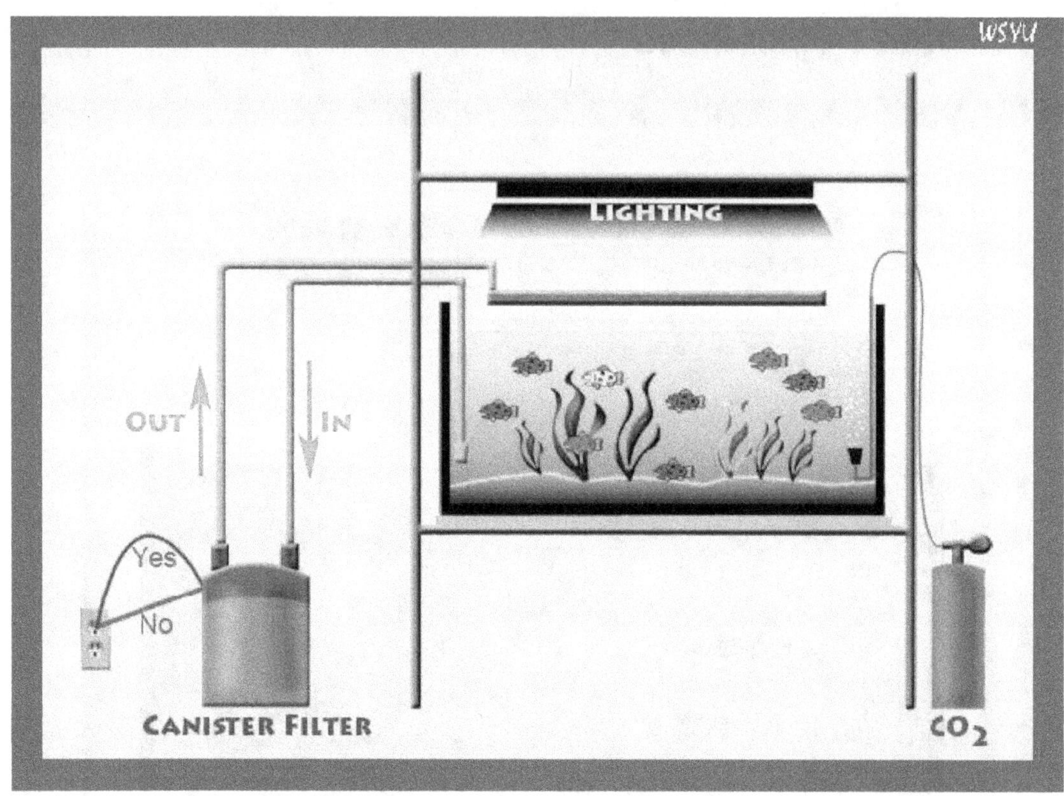

External Canister Filter for big aquariums and CO2 Supply for red plants

For bigger aquariums of 4 feet or 1.3 meter long or bigger, external canister water filters are used. They serve three purposes:

1. Capture solid waste from fish, excess food and plant debris.

2. Provide a place in the canister filter for the growth of beneficial bacteria. Such bacteria turn some of the toxic elements of ammonia and nitrite, produced by fish waste and decaying plants and food, into less hazardous elements.

3. Blend oxygen in the water when the water fall hit the water surface.

If you intend to keep a big variety of green and red plants, a CO2 system is essential. Plants need light and CO2. In particular, red plants need plenty of light and CO2. Similar to the lighting system, a timer is often used to switch the CO2 off at night.

External filters and CO2 systems are not essential if we keep the aquarium small, number of fish down, and adopt green plants that do not need a lot of light and CO2.

Just in case you really want a big aquarium and therefore need a canister filter, check two things before buying a canister filter:

1. Is the flow rate fast enough for your fish tank? A basic requirement is a flow rate of 3-5 times of the volume of water in your tank per hour. Check related specifications before making your buying decision.

2. The filter is normally filled completely with water. How easy it is to open for cleaning? Some models are very difficult. Check related online reviews before buying.

And just in case you want to try keeping red plants with a CO2 system, please consider two things:

1. DIY CO2 systems that use yeast cultures are troublesome and not cost effective in the long run.

2. Do you really have the time to trim your fast growing plants, due to a good CO2 supply, by taking most of them out of the water, trim the roots, and then put them back one by one every week?

Finally as a safety note, take a look at the lower left hand corner of the illustration above. Power cables should be arranged in such a way that accidental water dripping into the power plug along the power cable is not possible.

As depicted above, if we adopt green plants that are less demanding on CO2, we can do away with the CO2 system. We can even keep the plants growing well without planting them in aqua soil. If the aquarium is small enough, fish are not over stocked, and we do partial water change twice a week, we can do away with the use of any electric power driven water filter. We can simply use the smallest and least expensive kind of filter available. The air driven

sponge filter shown above provides the same 3 functions as its much bigger electric driven canister filter counterpart.

Breeding killies requires a means of egg collection. If the purpose is solely in the viewing of a colourful water world, one can freely decorate the fish tank in any style and in any way one likes. Otherwise, leave enough space in the aquarium for putting egg collecting bowls and mops.

The above is a simple one-foot bare bottom tank with one rock, two pieces of driftwood, and some easy plants called **Java Fern**. Java Fern stay healthy without strong light, CO2, or aqua-soil. There is a sponge filter, a heater for the winter, and a super small thermometer on the right hand side of the setup.

SETUP OF A TWO FOOT TANK

The above is a bigger two-foot bare bottom tank. At the middle of the tank, we have healthy fast growing **Java Moss** tied onto a piece of driftwood by fishing lines. Java Moss grow very quickly even under dim light without a CO2 system. If you are buying Java Moss, buy only the minimum selling quantity and let them multiply in your aquarium. Plenty of floating plants are put in the tank for softening the light for my fish. They feel safer with a lot of plants around too. The whole setup is very relaxing and a joy to watch when the lighting of the room is dimmed. As can be seen due to a higher water volume, a bigger sponge filter is used on the right hand side.

SETUP OF A THREE FOOT TANK

The above is a still bigger three foot tank. Black pebbles are used as the base substrate for the mood I intended to set. I am using also inexpensive internal sponge filters. Sponge filters could be cleaned in just a minute or two and they are good for small and medium size aquariums.

Above is a closer look of the setup at an angle. One driftwood W1, two plants P1 and P2, and six rocks R1 to R6. The tiny rock R4 at the front is there to keep the plant P1 in position. Plant P2 on the other hand needs no support as it is relatively heavy. Plant P1 is Java Fern that you have seen before and plant P2 is **Anubias Barteri**. Both of them stay healthy in dim light without extra CO2 supply and the use of aqua-soil. There is a miniature version of Anubias Barteri called **Anubias Petite**. They are excellent for smaller tanks. Unfortunately, they are many times more expensive.

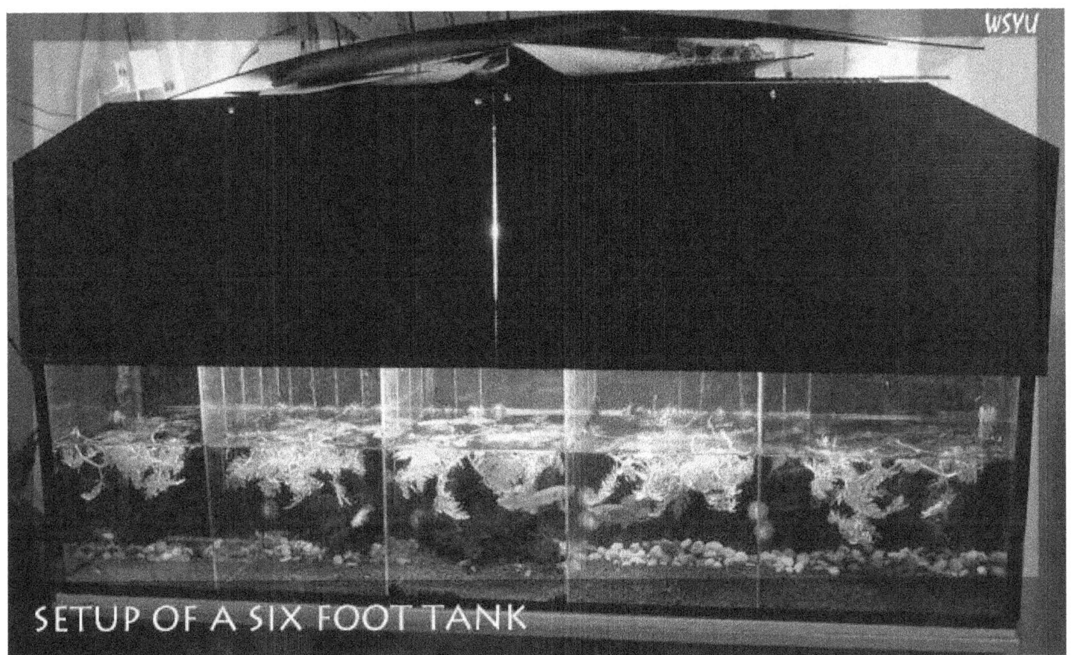

One can have a lot of fun decorating or aquascaping a big tank like the above six footer. For me however, I have too many fish and not enough space. In such a tank that use DIY dividers, make sure that every section is covered up properly with a net or cover. Killifish like to jump and if you do not cover up, they may jump and fall into their neighbouring sections. Strains of these species could be mixed if that happens.

One final thing to note about using a large tank like this is that the temperature at the end farthest away from the heater could be colder by 2-3 degrees in the winter.

Floating plants are important. Not only they subdue lights and create moods, they and their roots also provide shelters for the females or the weaker males from the dominant male in an aquarium. Recommended is **Amazon Frogbit** as shown on the upper right hand corner of the above photo. Don't buy a lot. Just buy the minimum selling quantity since they will multiply very quickly in your fish tank. As a side note, you can see a shrimp hiding out on top of a plant at the middle of the photo above. Killies love eating shrimps. Do not attempt to keep shrimps in a killie tank.

There is no need to feed any of the plants mentioned in this book. They will adapt well. DO NOT use plant nutrients. Also,do not use any thing of a chemical nature in a killifish tank eventhough they are intended for aquarium use. Killifish are very sensitive to chemicals. One may wipe the whole tank of killifish out overnight if not careful by adding just a few drops of any thing chemical.

Not all plants are aqua plants. Only aqua plants survive when submerged. Those that are not will die and decay rather quickly in water. For example, the plant shown in the above photo is not an aqua plant. I put it in for photographic purpose only as I was trying to bring out the colour of the fish. Name of this species: **Aphyosemion pyrophore Otto Gardneri**.

I prefer to have some corners of some of my tanks dim for the mood and for offering the fish a place to hide if they want to do so. In such tanks, those plants under good light will grow quite nicely while those at the dim corners won't. Part of such plants even starts to decay, though quite slowly. That is fine as long as the normal twice weekly partial water change is performed. There is no need to remove decaying parts from those plants unless you really want to. For me, I will leave them there for their natural looks.

2.3 Water Quality Requirements

Ideal temperature and water qualities may vary depending on the species. Some killies must have specific water qualities while many others can tolerate a wide range of temperature and water conditions, **as long as the change in temperature and water qualities is not sudden**. Luckily, most of the killies available to the general public are of the latter kind and it is therefore NOT necessary for you to measure and monitor closely any of such water qualities. All you need to do is to follow the same prescribed water conditioning and twice-a-week water changing routine to make water qualities good and stable.

Three basic water qualities will be discussed: acidity, hardness, and TDS. Again, **it is not necessary for you to measure any of these three water qualities.** They are described here just as you may want to know enough of these terms to appreciate exactly why and how you will have to condition the water and do partial water changes on schedule.

Acidity (pH): Our city tap water is well treated and mostly neutral with an acidity or pH range from 6.5 to 8.0. Most of the time, the pH value of the water from the tap is very stable at say 7.5. In nature, **clean water** could be neutral, alkaline or acidic. Most killies live in slightly acidic water with a pH of 5.5-6.5, caused by decaying organic matters like woods and plants. Some killie species, on the other hand, live in water that are alkaline with a pH of 7.5-8.0, due to the abundance of rocks and minerals.

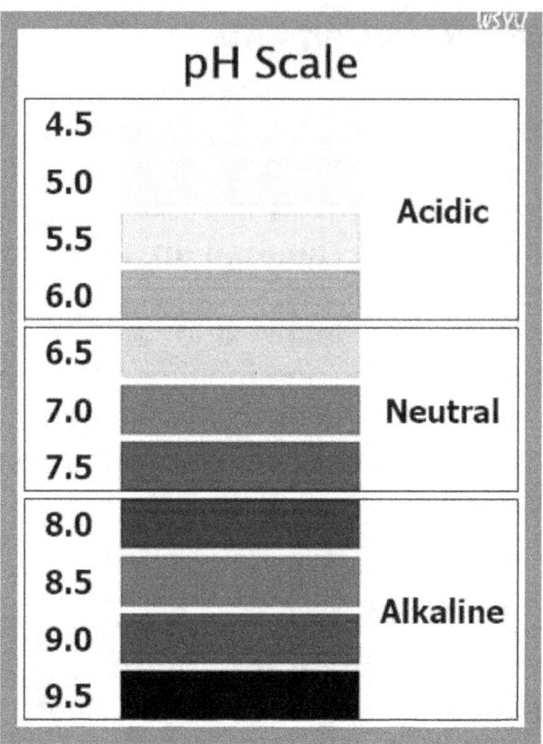

If you are curious and really want to do some tests, buy an inexpensive electronic pH meter. The cheapest ones could be available for less than USD10 online. Test the acidity of your tap water, water from your aquarium just after a partial water change, and water from your aquarium again 3 days later before the next partial water change. To keep the acidity or pH value of your water relatively stable, one need to do a 1/3 water change at least twice a week.

Each killifish species has its own set of ideal temperature and water quality. It would be very troublesome if not impossible even for professional breeders to fine tune the pH value of each aquarium for each species. Fortunately, the majority of killifish species could adapt very well to an environment change **if the change is not sudden**. This rule applies equally well to non-killifish as well. For all practical purposes, there is no need to check the acidity or other quality of your water if you do <u>water matching</u> before introducing fish into your aquarium and stick onto the same water conditioning and partial water change routine. Water conditioning will be covered in the next section and water matching in Chapter 3.

Hardness: Pure water, perhaps by distillation, has zero hardness and it is the softest of all. In the city, tap water contains traces of elements like calcium and magnesium ions and is harder. In the country, tap water originates from a well is harder still since water absorbs minerals while passing through the ground. However in modern rural homes, well water would have already been conditioned by a filter and a softener of some sorts for at least a partial removal of trace elements and odour before reaching the tap.

Most killifish prefer water in the slightly softer side but they are adaptive. As a results, no further filtration is required on our tap water. Water hardness is a lot more complex to measure than acidity. To simplify things for our practical application, we measure a third property called TDS instead. **TDS** or **Total Dissolved Solid** is the last water quality to discuss in this book. The lower the TDS in parts per million (PPM), the purer is the water. As the water get polluted by fish wastage and corroding food and plants, it gets less pure and its TDS get higher in value.

TDS in Parts Per Million (PPM)		
0-50		Filtered Water
50-100		Spring Water
100-200		Tap Water
200-300		
300-400		Water is Fine
400-500		Water Change
500+		Hazardous

Unlike water hardness, TDS could be measured easily with an inexpensive electronic tool. At this time of writing, a budget TDS meter is available for USD20 (plus freight) online. Below is a typical budget TDS meter:

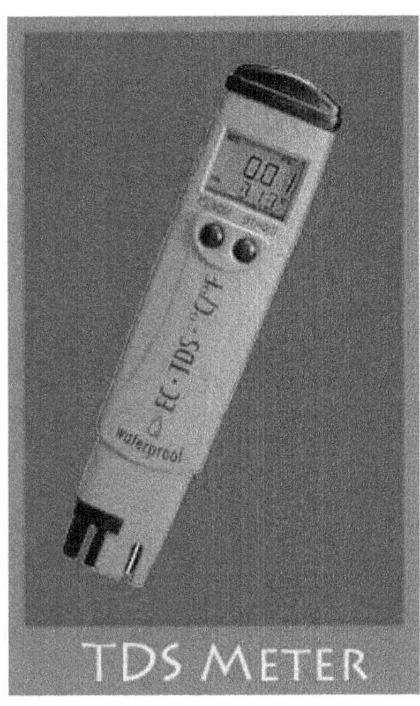

To measure, just turn it on and dip the tip into the water. Some TDS meters are not showing readings directly in PPM. e.g. one may have to multiply the readout by five to get the TDS readings in PPM. Read the user manual before use.

My tap water has a low TDS of 125-150 PPM and therefore, so is the water in a freshly setup tank. This TDS value will increase by the hours due to fish waste, excess food and plant debris. At the end of the week while the water **still look absolutely clear and clean**, the reading could have approached an amazingly high of 500 PPM, which is hazardous to both fish and human. A one third water change every three days or twice weekly will keep the TDS down to a maximum level of around 300 PPM.

If you want to take a simple look into water quality or purity, and appreciate better why you have to do partial water change twice a week and not just once a week, buy a TDS meter. Otherwise, you don't have to use one. **All you have to do is to follow the rules of:**

1. **Allocate 1.5 gallon of water per pair of fish.**
2. **Two 1/3 water changes a week with conditioned water.**

One important final note: even if the TDS meter reading is extremely high, say much higher than 500 pm, your fish will not die or look particularly bad or ill. They will just live a much shorter life and lay less eggs. Fish bought from irresponsible pet stores or sellers may look good upon arrival but if the fish were not treated right, they could die very soon in your tank no matter how good you take care of them.

2.4 Water Conditioning

Even though further filtration on our tap water is not needed, we have to get rid of the chlorine. Chlorine is added to our drinking water to eliminate harmful bacteria for human consumption. However, chlorine is toxic to fish, plants and the beneficial bacteria. We eliminate chlorine from the tap water by exposing it to the air overnight. A water storage bin is therefore needed. For convenience, I keep water ready in the bin all the time.

Although killies can adapt to the acidity and hardness of the tap water, we take the opportunity of water sitting in the bin overnight to fine tune the acidity and hardness. We can change the water acidity and hardness in many ways. For example, by putting dried almond leaves in the water and let them decay. An added benefit could be the colouring of water. A tint of green could give the aquarium a natural look, as below.

Dried Almond Leaves In An Aquarium for ELB N'tui

Using dried almond leaves could be difficult as the more they decay, the more acidic the water will become. For ease of maintenance, we want to avoid the task of measuring water quality. We will therefore use something a lot more stable, like peat pellets.

Most killifish prefer the water to be slightly acidic and less hard, say for a pH of 5.5-6.5. To do this, put a cloth bag of Peat Pellets or Aqua Soil, available online or from your local pet shops, in your water storage bin or bucket. Peat pellet not only is acidic by itself, it interacts chemically with the calcium and magnesium ions and soften the water. Replace the peat pellets twice a year.

If we need to condition our water to be more alkaline and hard, say for a pH of 7.5 to 8.0 for Lamprichthys Tanganicanus, use a bag of Crushed Coral or Marine Sand, available also online or from your local pet shops, in your water storage bin or bucket. Crushed coral and sand must be cleaned before use. Rinse them until the water turns from cloudy to clear. Replace them also twice a year.

You can do a simple test if you have an acidity test kit. I put peat pellet in one cup of tap water and pebbles into another overnight and then compared. My tap water has a acidity or pH of 7.4. Much to our expectation, pebbles did nothing to the water quality. Peat pellet on the other hand lowered the pH value to 6.0, making it more acidic. Tested again after a few more days and the values didn't change much further. Peat pellet is a much better water conditioning media for us than almond leaves as its effect is very much predictable.

Almond leaves are still useful if we want to fine tune the water quality for a particular species that require extra acidity or when we want to colour the water.

Below shows what I did to condition the water. I was using peat pellets in one bin for most of my killies and crushed coral in another bin just for my Lamprichthys Tanganicanus. Tap water is added and stored at least overnight to eliminate the chlorine. I replaced the substrate about twice a year.

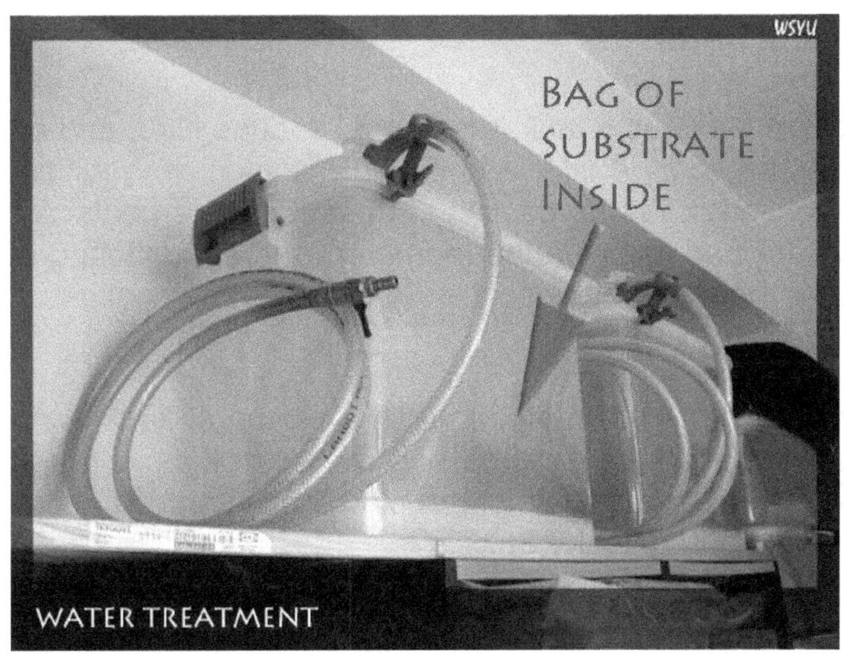

I put my water conditioning bins near the ceiling. Water changes is tidy, quick, and easy.

2.5 Step-by-Step Setup

The basic hardware includes a tank, an internal sponge filter, and an air pump to drive the sponge filter and provide oxygen. In addition, we provide the lighting, a fan for cooling in the summer, a heater for heating in the winter and finally, a thermometer for the monitoring of temperature. All of these will be described in the following sections.

An important requirement to remember is to cover up all tanks with lids or nets. Many killies love to jump and they can jump through extremely fine gaps in the lids or nets. Keeping the water level really low is workable but not practical.

The biggest mistake often made by beginner fish keepers, killifish or any fish, is keeping too many fish in one aquarium. Unless water change is very frequent and fully automatic, we just cannot keep too many fish. Ideally for our home setup, 1 to 1.5 gallon of clean water per pair of adult 5-cm long killifish is required. Bigger species will need more space and water. Fish will be under stress if such requirement is not met and needless to say, it would be harder to keep them healthy if they are stressed. A one foot tank may therefore ideally house only two pairs or one trio of killies. One trio means one male and 2 females. Ideally for breeding purpose, females should out number males by a good margin. The table below is a guide to some tank sizes and their water volume and weight.

Aquarium Size Examples		Volume of Water (80% Full)		Water Weight (80% Full)		Max Pair of Fish
cm	inch	Liter	US Gallon	kg	lb	
30x20x23	12x8x9	11	3	11	24	2
41x21x26	16x8x10	18	5	18	39	3
30x30x30	12x12x12	22	6	22	48	4
60x30x36	24x12x14	52	14	52	114	9
53x29x44	21x12x18	54	14	54	119	10
90x45x45	36x18x18	146	38	146	321	26

All Figures Rounded

1 US Gallon has 3.79 Liter

1 Liter Water weighs 1 kilogram or 2.20 pound

Ideal Water Volume for One Pair of Killifish is 1.5 Gallon

Tank sizes have no standards and the guide above serves as a quick reference of two things.

1. Don't keep more fish than the stocking density shown. Less space per pair would mean higher stress and the fish will be more prone to illness. Also, water quality will become less stable.

2. Water is very heavy. The tank, pebbles, and rocks are heavy too. The stand or shelving must be strong enough so that it won't collapse or topple.

If not for breeding, select the largest size of aquarium that your space and budget will allow. This will provide more stable water quality, greater choice of fish and plants, and an enhanced aesthetic value. Put the tank away from direct sunlight as sunlight can lead to unwanted algae growth in the tank and the decorations. For breeding, a smaller setup will make egg collection easier.

Let's start now with the step by step setup of an aquarium!

A. Protect areas around the aquarium from water evaporation damage with plastic wrap. This is extremely important even if you intend to put a lid on your tank.

B. Install lighting. I prefer fluorescent tube batten and I secure them with cable ties. They are a lot cheaper than those that are built specifically for fitting on top of an aquarium. The space between the tank and the batten is also adjustable when we DIY. Tight space between the lighting batten and the tank will make routine maintenance difficult. Allow as big a gap as possible. In general, keep the light on ten hours a day. If you find algae growing, reduce the time. If your plants do not look too healthy, try twelve hours a day. Use a budget timer to turn the light on and off at the same time each day.

C. Wash the aquarium, sponge filter, and rocks briefly with salt and water. Do not use detergents or chemicals of any kind. Do not use cloth and bucket that have been exposed to detergent. At this stage, there is no need to rinse the interior with fresh water. Wipe the outside of the tank dry with a piece of cloth or newspaper.

D. Glass is brittle and will break if a water filled tank is put on an uneven hard surface or for example an even hard surface but with a grain of sand on it. Always pad the tank with something even and soft, like a sheet of Styrofoam or cardboard. In the setup above, I put the tank on top of a sheet of cardboard.

E. Clean all driftwood by boiling them in water. One may have to repeat the process until the water becomes relatively clear. A light tint, however, could be preferable by both the observers and the fish. Boiling will also make driftwood sink in water and stay at the bottom. If your piece of driftwood floats, boil them again in hot water. Driftwood comes in different shapes and sizes and are priced accordingly. Do not buy unless you have a decoration design already in mind.

F. Put everything, except the plants and fish, in the tank and fill it up close to the top with water. Add a lot of salt and let everything soak and sterilize for a day or two. In the above, I have a stone, two pieces of driftwood, one sponge filter and an air stone. The air stone will be used in another tank for hatching eggs. I was putting the air stone inside for sterilization purpose only. Do not buy any fish or plant until everything is set up.

G. It is now a very good time to try different decoration layouts when the fish and plants are not there. Play with the rocks and driftwood.

H. It is of utmost importance to verify that the tank does not leak before you leave!

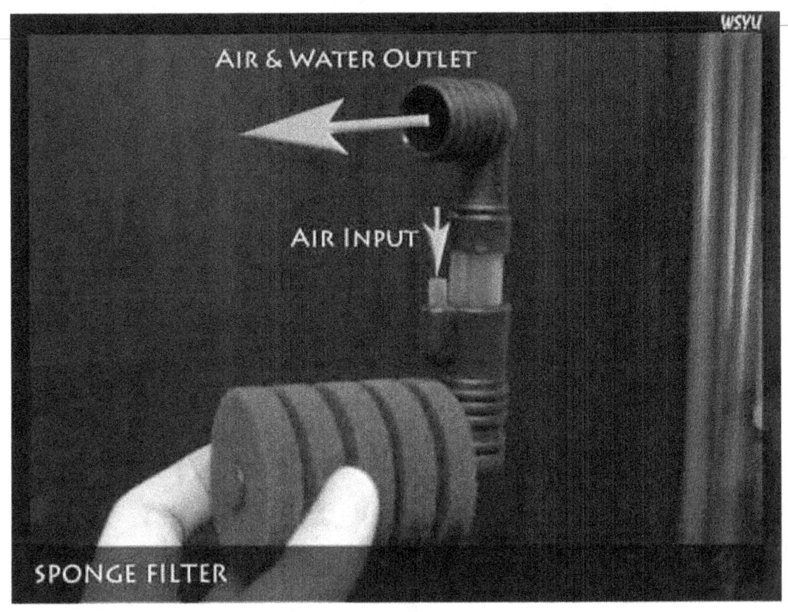

All Sponge Filters Work On The Same Principle

I. Sponge filters work with air pumps. As shown above, air is injected into the air input opening with a plastic air line. The air then escapes through the outlet at the top at a high speed. The escape of air sucks in water through the sponge and as a result, the sponge filters the water going through it. The sponge serves also as a home for the beneficial bacteria that clean the water. **Rinse the sponge briefly with water from the same fish tank once a month to get rld of the solid waste.** The whole cleaning process will only take a minute or two. If you rinse the sponge with water other than that from the fish tank, the beneficial bacteria may very likely die.

The air escaping from the top outlet stir up the water surface. Oxygen is blended in the water through this process.

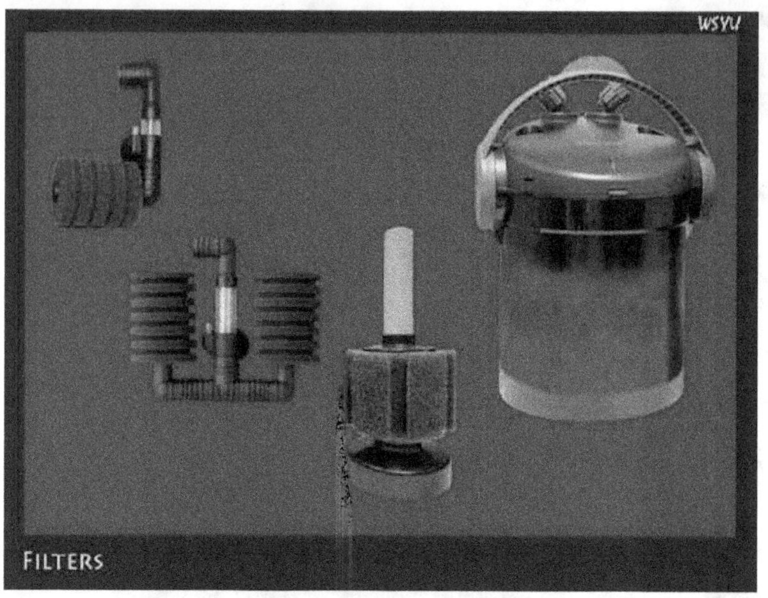

J. The size of the sponge filter increases with the volume of water as in general, one keeps more fish in bigger tanks and more waste is created. The smallest filter shown above on the left is good for tanks up to 2 foot in size and the middle two filters are good for 3 foot tanks. 4 foot or bigger tanks would need external canister filters of different sizes.

The use of under-gravel filtration systems is not recommended. Cleaning them requires the tearing down of the whole decoration.

A Dual-Nozzle Low-Noise Air Pump With Volume Control

K. It is a good idea to spend a few more dollars on a less noisy "quiet" air pump. It makes keeping fish much more enjoyable. An optional air volume control (the knob on the top right hand side of the photo above) will be nice. If you plan to have more than one tank, multiple nozzle pumps for multiple air line connections will be needed.

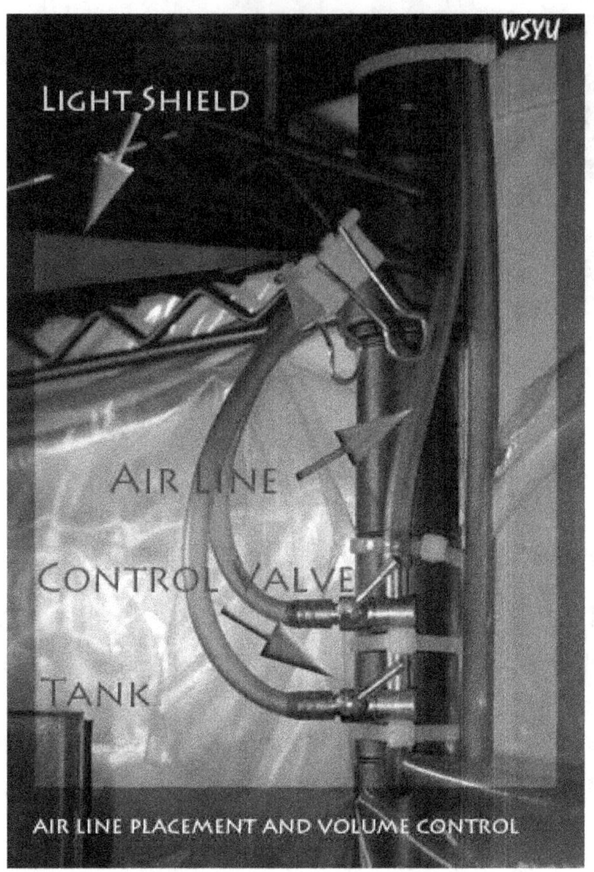

L. Even if your air pump has volume control, we need to put an air valve in every air line that feed each sponge filter or air stone for fine tuning the air flow. This is required as the distance from the air pump to each sponge filter is different. The longer the air line, the more the resistance to the flow of air.

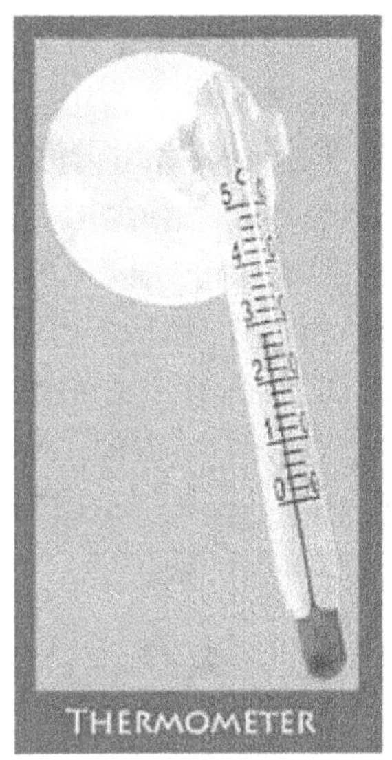

M. Find the smallest available thermometer to save on precious aquarium real estate. They are cheaper as well. Don't use sticker type as they don't show accuracy to the degree.

Ensure that water has been conditioned.

N. Siphon out all the salty water after a day or two. Add water that has been seasoned at least overnight according to the simple instructions in section <u>2.4</u>. Put everything back in. Put the plants in as well and turn the air pump on. Absolutely no fish allowed until the while setup is done. If time is available, you may set the tank now. If not, come back until you are ready. Unlike the previous step of cleaning, we do not fill up close to the rim. Leave about two inches of space. Most killifish love to jump and it helps to reduce loss with a lower level of water. After all, there is time when we have to leave the lid open for feeding or maintenance.

O. The simple aquascaping is done and the tank is now set! If you prefer, buy a long pair of tongs of say 12 inch long for inserting the plants between rocks.

P. Cover the three sides of each tank up with plastic sheets to give the fish a greater sense of security. Colour of blue or black looks best to me and I used blue in this case.

Q. I hang plastic sheets before the fluorescent lighting. They block unwanted light from entering my eyes when viewing and from entering my lens when taking photos. The DIY light shield can easily be flipped out and clipped into position for feeding or maintenance.

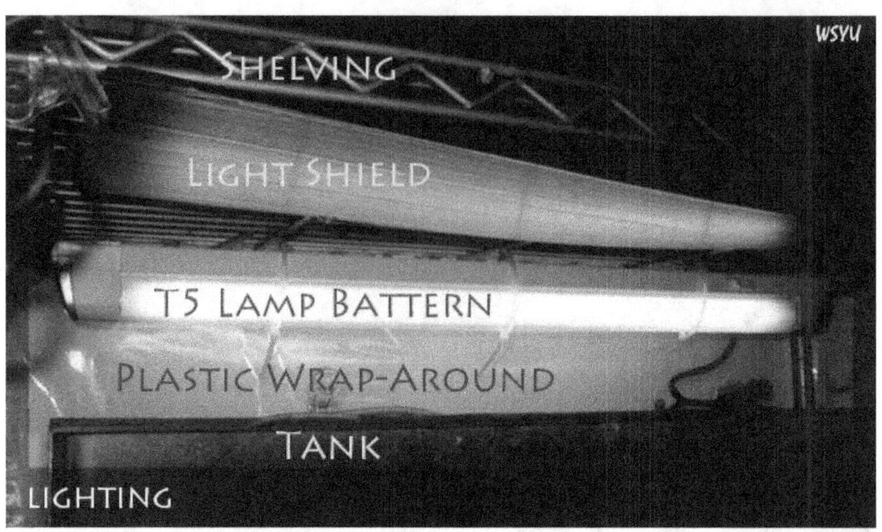

R. The above is a closer look when the light shield is flipped open.

S. For the most common kinds of killifish like RAC and AUS, water temperature anywhere between 20-30 degree Celsius or 68-86 degree Fahrenheit is good. They will survive outside of that temperature range but that is not desirable. You should check the temperature requirement of the fish that you want to buy online before buying. Water coolers are a lot more expensive than heaters and you may want to avoid those fish that need very cool water. For heaters, buy only fully submersible and shatter-proof ones. They are just a little bit more expensive. Wattage of heater depends on the volume of your tank. Check heater specification before buying. In normal use with fish inside the tank, adjust the heater temperature in several small steps until the desired temperature is reached. Too rapid a temperature change in one step could kill the fish.

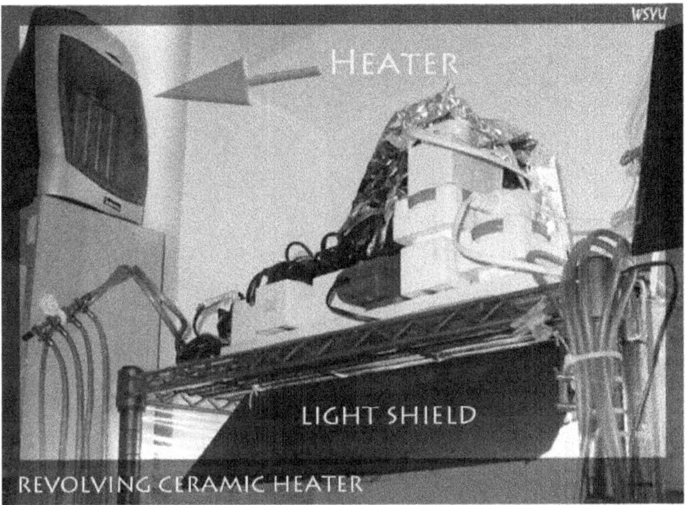

A Ceramic Heater in the Fish Room.

T. As shown above, depending on the number of tanks that one has, it might be a lot more cost effective to heat up the whole room with one heater. For me with many tanks, I put the heater and power bar on top of the shelf to prevent water from spilling onto it by accident.

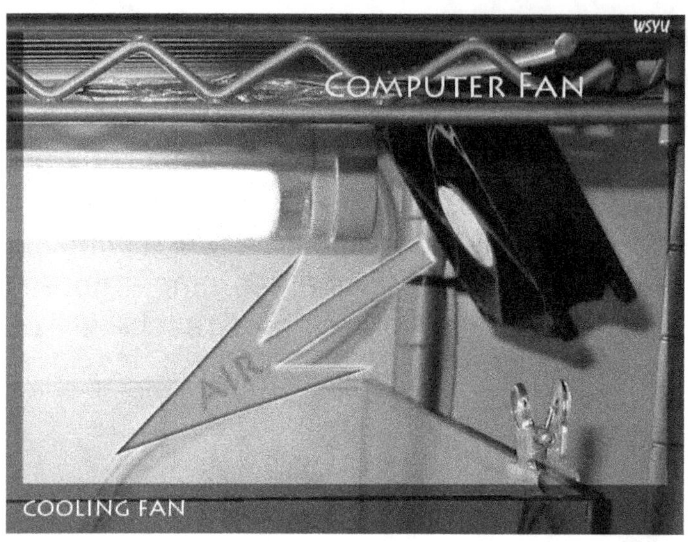

Water Cooling By Evaporation.

U. As shown above, a small 2-inch or 5-cm DC computer fan is a cost effective means of cooling the water down in the summer. It can cool a one-foot tank down by 2-3 degrees. One small AC to DC adapter may drive several of such fans. Check the specifications of both the fan and power adapter before buying. Do not exceed the maximum current supply specification of the adapter. For example, an AC to DC power adapter with a specification of 1A or 1000 mA can drive a maximum of 5 computer fans that draws 0.2A or 200 mA each. If you have many tanks, consider cooling the whole room with a window air conditioner. If you can afford it and don't want the whole room cool, buy a water cooler.

The bare base aquarium is now ready and you may now go buy your fish. Don't ever bring the fish home when your aquarium is not ready.

V. Substrate: I use mostly bare base tanks for the ease of maintenance and egg collection. One such setup is shown above for breeding **Aphyosemion ogoense GHP 80-23**. If there is no need for you to collect every single egg, **feel free to use any kind of substrate at the bottom** and make your aquarium pretty! Clean substrate well as if they are rocks before putting them in the aquarium.

One may use peat pellet as the substrate as shown above. They give you a nice brown colour bottom. Peat pellets condition water quality too, as was explained in section 2.4. Replace peat pellets twice a year. If they have to be moved from one tank to another, sterilize them by rinsing and boiling in hot water. Killie in the photo: **Fundulopanchax gresensi Takwai.**

Do check the package label that the peat pellets do not contain fertilizers or chemicals before buying. If such kinds are used, killifish will die in just a few hours.

Pebbles and sand are of course very common substrates. When new, rinse them until water turns from milky to clear. Add salt and soak overnight before putting them into your aquarium. For ease of maintenance, avoid using light colour pebbles and sand. They will get dirty very quickly and will no longer look good in just a week or two. Killie in the photo: **Aphyosemion exiguum Zouatopsi**.

In the above setup, I put black sand on top of peat pellets. Unlike pebbles, finer sand make live food like worms harder to get under the substrate and water quality will be easier to maintain. In the end, it will be you to decide what substrate to use in terms of look and function. For sand and pebbles, remove and rinse them with salt at least every six month, or whenever you are re-decorating the aquarium. Killie in the photo: **Aphyosemion decorsei Kapou RCA 91-1**.

We may also use loose substrate like Sphagnum Moss and Dried Peat Moss for the special look of them.

In the above setup, I used very inexpensive Sphagnum Moss for gardening as the bottom substrate. There are two types, with or without fertilizers. Check the labelling before you buy. Any fertilizer or chemical will kill your fish in just a few hours. Name of killie: **Chromaphyosemion splendopleure Ekondo Titi**

Sphagnum moss came dried. They will expand several times bigger after soaking in water. Their orange and yellow colour go nicely with some killifish.

Brown peat moss is used as the substrate in the above setup. The main difference from the other substrates is again that they are loose. Dirt gets under them easily. Feed slowly and do not overfeed is key to keep the substrate clean. The fish called **PCR** in this case is a peat diver. He will not mate on the substrate as the peat moss layer is too shallow for them to dive completely into. I used peat moss in this setup simply because I love the look of it. If I want them to mate and collect eggs, I will give them also a tall bowl or cup of peat moss.

Peat moss are available in bulk or in brand named boxes. Check that they do not contain any fertilizer before buying. Dried peat moss will not sink in water by themselves. They must be boiled in water for a few minutes before use, as follows:

Don't put peat moss into the aquarium until they have fully cooled down. Unlike pebbles or sand, do not attempt to clean and reuse used peat moss. Remove Peat Moss or Sphagnum Moss weekly to check for eggs.

W. DIY clear dividers could be useful at times. Make sure that water can flow through by cutting slits or holes in the dividers. Dividers are used for two purposes. The first one is to prevent fighting among fish of the **same** species if they are rare or before their delivery to their new owners. Killie in the photo: **Nematolebias papilliferous**.

In the instance above, the divider separates two **different** species when we run out of tanks. The two **SJO** may look alike but they are of different strains. As mentioned before, we do not encourage cross breeding even between two similar species. Cover each section up very carefully with a net as killifish like to jump once in a while.

2.6 Routine Maintenance

Water Change: It is very important that you do two 1/3 water changes a week. If siphoning water out of your tank manually, I recommend using battery operated siphons. They are just a little more expensive but they will save you a lot of time and trouble. Remove any solid waste, excess food, or any debris that you see when siphoning. There is no need to stir things up. Just pick up what is obvious along the way.

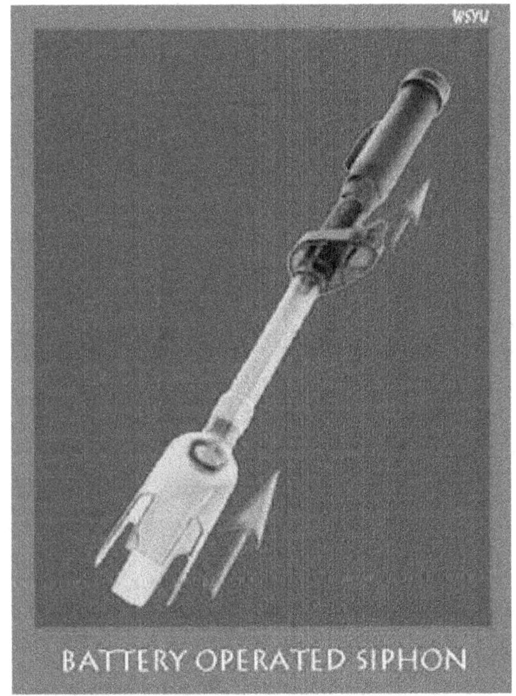

Glass Cleaning: We can clean an aquarium, even with water and fish in it with a clean sponge. A plastic card is also very useful. Do the cleaning just before a partial water change. If cleaning the tank by itself, as below, use some salt. Do NOT use any chemical or detergent.

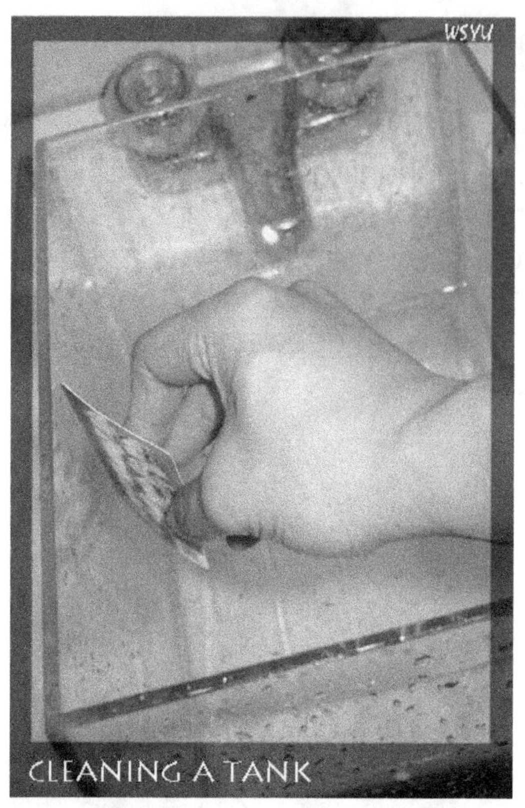

Sponge Filter Cleaning: Beneficial bacteria reside on the sponge. We do not want to kill them as it will take a few days to build them up again. Monthly, stop the air pump and take the sponge filter out, slide the sponge out and rinse it with some water from the same tank until most of the solid waste is gone. Put the filter quickly back in the tank. Drying the sponge out will also kill the beneficial bacteria. The same is true for external canister filter. Use only water from the aquarium for rinsing the filter materials inside the canister.

2.7 Budget of Hobby

This is for your quick reference to see what is good to have for a two-foot aquarium. Prices are for reference only. You may want to know now that you can subsidize or even reclaim all such costs by selling some of the eggs that you are going to collect. Collecting and selling eggs are a great part of the fun in keeping killifish.

Estimated Price in USD. Freight is Extra.		Description	Must Have
Aquarium	50	One 24-inch glass tank with lid. Smaller is OK.	Yes
Sponge Filter	3	One Twin-sponge Filter	Yes
Air Pump	10	Air Pump for a 30 gallon Tank	Yes
Fluorescent Lighting	30	4-foot 2-tube Fluorescent Lighting Fixture	Yes
Timer	15	For turning the light on/off.	Optional
Thermometer	2	Not self-sticking	Yes
Air-line, Air Stone, Air Control Valve.	10	A kit of 25-ft air-line, 4 air stones, 4 tees, 5 tee air control valves.	Yes
Fish Net	3	Smallest Size	Yes
Siphon	14	Battery Operated.	Yes
Heater	20	50-Watt Submersible	Optional
Cooling Fan	15	Twin-fan with DC Power	Optional

		Adapter	
Sand	19	One inch layer of black sand for the 2-foot tank, about 16-lb or 7-kg.	Optional
Pebble	4	Half an inch for the 2-foot tank. About 5-lb or 2-kg.	Optional
Driftwood	5 up	8-inch long, price dependent on shape.	Optional
Plants	10	Spend at least $10 on them.	Yes
Peat Pellet	6	500g to put in water storage bin	Yes
Water Storage Bin	22	18 gallon storage bin	Yes
pH Meter	10	Inexpensive budget Acidity meter	Optional
TDS Meter	20	Inexpensive budget TDS meter	Optional

Chapter Two Highlight

- Store water in a bin with an optional bag of peat pellet at least overnight. Do a 1/3 partial water change twice a week. Do not skip a water change. Just in case you skipped, change no more than 1/3 of the water at a time. Stability is everything. Water may look clear and clean but in fact not so.

- There is no need to measure water qualities like acidity, hardness, or TDS unless in the rare case that you have a very special species. Do measure water temperature and adjust if necessary.

- Any rapid change of water qualities will drastically shorten the life of fish without them showing any obvious sign of illness.

Fundulopanchax sjoestedti Dwarf Blue VAKA

WSYU
SIMPSONICTHYS FULMINANTIS

Chapter 3
Buying & Keeping Killies

Chapter 3: Buying & Keeping Killifish

3.1 Make A Wish List

One can only buy what is available currently on the market but still, make a wish list! From my back up hard disk drive, I still have my original wish list back in 2004, before I started keeping any of them.

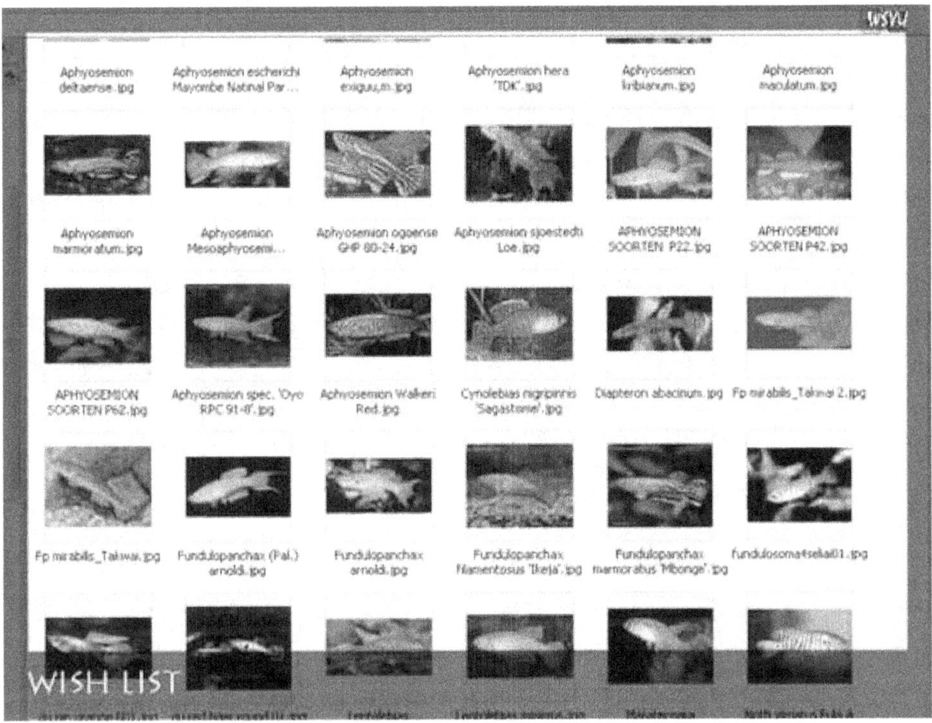

Out of this list, I would still like to try Fundulopanchax sjoestedti Loe, Aphyosemion caudofasciatum, and Aphyosemion soorten.

3.2 Fish Buying

You can buy live fish from your local shops, pick-up at the home of a local seller, or buy them online. One popular online source is Aquabid.com. The same Web site is also popular for buying and selling eggs. Egg buying and selling will be discussed in section 6.1.

Pet Shop - While people are normally selling killifish in pairs online, pet shops may quite likely sell only the males. Females could be harder to come by as new born killifish are mostly males. Also, pet shops are more likely to mix similar species together to save on tank real estate. Worst, they may save the time and effort of water matching before releasing the fish into their tanks. Water matching is discussed in section 3.4 below. As you may already know by now, a sudden change in water quality will drastically shorten the lifespan of a fish. Therefore, it is advisable to buy only from reputable sources and read supplier reviews online.

Pick up at Local Breeder's Home - That would be great as you will have a chance to meet a new friend and learn from him or her. Again, check if reviews about these sellers are available before you buy from them.

Online Purchasing - A pair or a trio will normally be on offer and that is nice. Just like any online buying, check customer feedback first. Never pay cash or release you credit card information to the seller. In my experience, PayPal is quite secure and reliable. In case something goes wrong with the seller, PayPal will help and get your money back rather quickly.

After placing your order and knowing when your fish will likely arrive, prepare to get your tank and water ready for your fish at least a day or two earlier. If it is possible, avoid working overtime when the fish arrive. Conditioning the fish with the water in your tank i.e. water matching, could take a lot of time and you don't want to stay awake at night doing that.

3.3 Fish Arrival

Lamprichthys Tanganicanus arrived in normal plastic bags.

Normal plastic bags are not breathable. In a sealed bag of fish, about 1/3 of the volume is water, the rest is either air or oxygen. Oxygen is a lot more expensive than air and it is used normally for more expensive species and for longer distance shipments only. To prevent fish waste from fouling the precious air and water in the bag and killing the fish, the fish are normally put to a fast for at least a day before bagging for the shipment.

Don't blind your fish by opening your fish parcel all of a sudden in bright light. They have been in the dark for a very long time. Gradually give them more light by covering them up in complete darkness first. Give them 30 minutes or more for adjusting in steps from total darkness to normal lighting.

If you buy locally from a pet shop or seller, bring the new fish home as soon as possible and avoid temperature changes.

At this stage, you may "float" the bag by simply putting the bag of fish in their intended aquarium to slowly achieve a temperature match. Water matching will be described in the next section.

If DOA, or death on arrival, do not open the bag. Take a clear photo of the fish and the unopened bag and send the photo to your seller the same day you receive your fish for a claim. Depending on the terms and agreement, the seller may have to send you replacement fish while you will be paying for the freight again. If the fish has started decaying, quiet likely the fish was dead very earlier in the journey. The fish was not too healthy to start with. Healthy fish could still be very lively after a journey of over one week.

As long as it is not freezing or hotter than 35 °C or 95°F, they would stay fine after a long journey of a few days. Still, I would recommend limiting the journey to no more than 5 days by using more expensive services.

Kordon Breathable Bag Has Special Markings On It. **Aphyosemion decorsei Kapou RCA 91-1** arrived in good shape after a journey of 8,000 miles.

More expensive Kordon breathing bags that allow the inflow of oxygen and outflow of carbon dioxide are getting popular with fish shippers. There is no longer a need to fill the bag with air or oxygen. Shipping volume is decreased by 2/3 and the saving in postage easily compensate the extra cost in using Kordon bags.

Unlike normal plastic bag inside which air or oxygen is added, **do not float sealed Kordon bags** for temperature matching. If you put the bag in your aquarium, the fish will suffocate. Oxygen gets into a Kordon bag only when the bag is in contact with the atmosphere.

3.4 Water Matching

One may be tempted to measure water parameters like acidity and hardness of the water in the bags, especially if you ordered several different species at the same time. After all, each killies species has its own preferred water parameters and such parameters are also clearly listed at the seller's website. The results? Different species that needs acidic water are sharing the same kind of acidic water while different species that needs alkaline water are sharing the same kind of alkaline water. These professional breeders are not adjusting water parameters for each species. They just don't have the time and resources to do so.

That, of course, is a relief. It simply confirms that killies are quite adaptive to water with different acidity and hardness. However, one must give them a few hours to slowly adapt. A process of water matching is required before you put the fish into your tank.

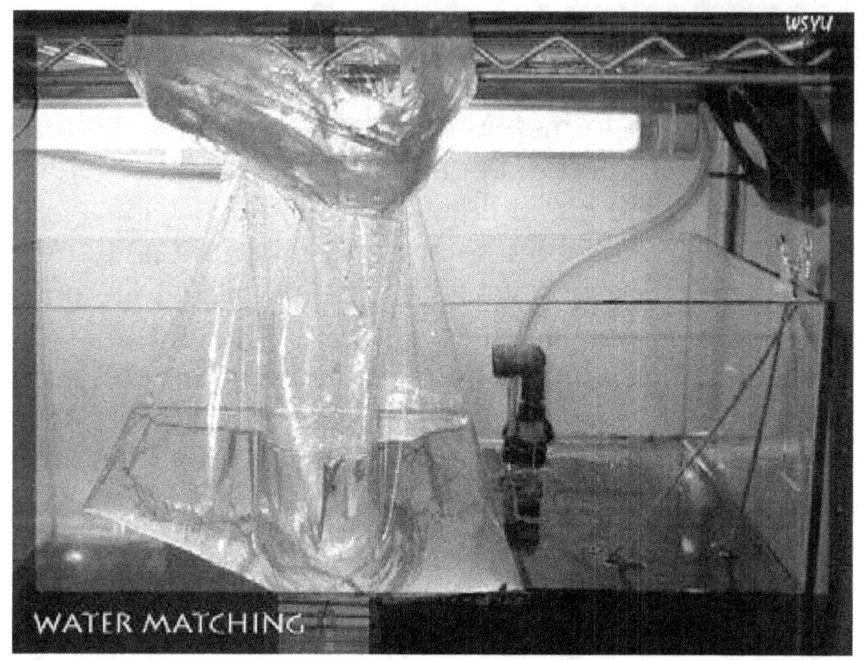

If the fish come in a regular plastic bag and water only occupy 1/3 of the space, use it for water matching. If they come in a Kordon bag, the bag will be too small. Transfer the fish and the water that comes with it to a bigger bag.

Open and hang the bags in front of the aquarium that you intend to put them in. If the water in the aquarium is different from room temperature as normally would in the winter, float part of the bag in the aquarium for a temperature match.

Now add water from the aquarium to the bag. Amount of water to add is about one third the amount of the water in the bag. Wait 30 minutes and add the same amount of water from the aquarium again. Repeat the step 5 more times. Discard part of the water in the bag if it became too full. Close the bag opening after each addition of water to avoid fish jumping right out. The whole water matching process will take two and a half hours if you remember to do every step on time. Do not start water matching very late at night or else you will have to go to bed very late.

Finally, scoop the fish into your aquarium. Discard all water in the bag as a preventive measure against possible disease from the seller's water. Some buyers will even put their newly arrived fish into quarantine tanks for the best possible protection of their existing fish. Do that if your resources allow.

3.5. Aggression

Killifish aggression has already been discussed in section 1.6. Power balance in your aquarium may change after new fish are introduced. Pay attention if any fish, existing or a new member, needs extra shelter for hiding. If necessary, remove the existing dominant fish for a while. Let the new fish adapt for a while in his new home before reintroducing the existing dominant fish would normally help.

Finally for newly arrived fish, it might be normal if they are not eating. Just don't disturb them. I have seen new fish not eating for a whole week. They just take longer than normal to adapt.

3.6. Disease

Watch also for illness that might have been brought along by the new fish.

In the above instance, the "fungus" exploded from within the fish the next day after arrival. (Name of killie: **Aphyosemion pyrophore Komono Yellow**) I had a new aquarium setup just for him and it was therefore very likely caused by a disease that he had already been carrying. He died the following day and I have never seen similar diseases again.

It is now a good time to describe the most common fish diseases and their possible treatments. Just don't forget that killifish are very sensitive to chemicals. The only thing that you should add to your aquarium is salt. Illnesses will not be common if you provide your fish with high water quality, proper temperature and lighting, proper feeding, and a lot of space.

Velvet Disease - It is the most common disease that you will see. The fish body is covered by a dusty coating with a colour anything from white to light brown. Normally by the time you see it, more than one fish will be infected. Treatment is rather easy by adding salt from your kitchen. One teaspoon per gallon of water should be enough. They will normally recover in a few days. Normally at the very early stage, the fish rub against hard objects trying to remove the parasites. When that happens, just add a little bit of salt. Quite likely, you were not doing a good housekeeping job. Keep a closer eye on the water quality and temperature.

White Spot Disease - It is also caused by parasites and not life threatening. Tiny white spots can be seen easily on the body and fins. Normally by the time you see it, more than one fish will be infected. Very slowly increase the water temperature to 30-32°C (86-90°F) and hold it there until the parasites die and the white spots fall off from the fish. Think stability all the time. Increase the temperature of the heater in 15 minute or longer steps of one degree each. Never turn the heater all the way to 30-32°C (86-90°F) in one step or else the fish may die.

Scale Protrusion and/or Belly Bloating - The unfortunate one in the below photo had both. Unlike the other two kinds of disease that could infect many fish at the same time, you will normally find only one fish suffering. Unfortunately, the chance of recovery is low. Do a partial water change, add salt, and hope for the best is all you can do. Again, good house keeping would greatly reduce the chance of fish having disease like these.

Scale Protrusion with Belly Bloating

End of Chapter Three

WSYU
NOTHOBRANCHIUS KAFUENSIS KAYUNI ZAM 97-9

WSYU
SIMPSONICTHYS WHITEI

Chapter 4. Breeding Killifish

4.1 Sex Ratio and Born Defects

Eggs just don't hatch to give a male and female ratio of close to one. The sex ratio of newborns quite often is so skewed that there are many more males than females. Sometimes, you don't even get one female.

This particular hatch of **PCR** shown above is male only!

Some examples of born defects that I have come across include fish swimming upside down and sideway, as above. Name of killie: **MAG**.

The **Nothobranchius furzeri MZM 04-3** above was born with only one side of gill membranes.

Finally, the most commonly seen born symptom is belly sliding. Belly sliders have trouble keeping afloat. Obviously, they have to work a lot harder to stay alive. Unlike the female in the photo above, the majority of belly sliders die at a very young age.

As of today, there is no sure way of sex ratio control or born defect prevention.

4.2 Egg Collection for Non-Annuals

Non-annuals, the nonseasonal killies, lay eggs almost everywhere.
Name of killie: **Aphyosemion australe Orange**.

However, if they are given a choice, non-annuals will more likely lay eggs on plants.

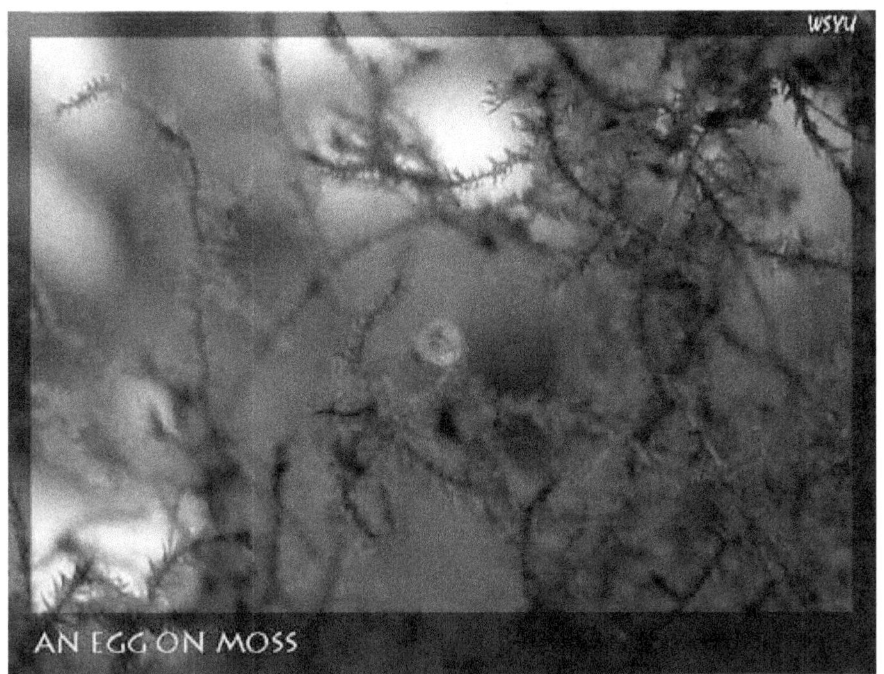

This Java Moss is still in water in the tank. Eggs on them are very hard to spot due to the complex shape of natural plants.

APHYOSEMION AUSTRALE ORANGE

To collect eggs, we give them plant-like mops. Some killies prefer to lay eggs at the top while some prefer the bottom more. It is therefore easier for us to provide them with a long mop hanging all the way from the top to the very bottom of the tank. Mops are made of nylon or acrylic yarn. Do not use wool or cotton as they will deteriorate in water. Like dried peat moss, microwave your mops in water before using. Pick any colour that you like or use whatever colour that you have on hand.

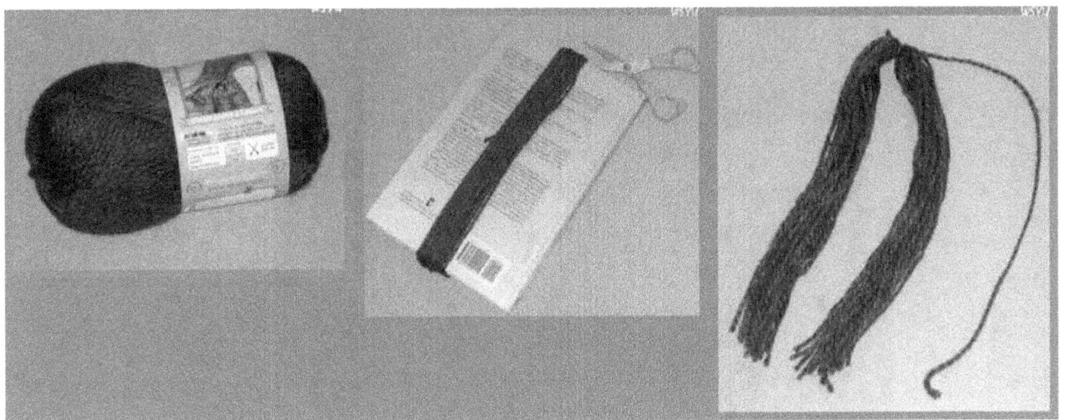

Mop making is easy. Just use whatever colour is available.

Just in case you don't have to collect every single egg, you don't have to remove all plants from the tank, as above.

In the above case, I sink a mop in just to try my luck. If I need to collect the majority of eggs that they produce,   I will isolate a pair or a trio of the fish in a plant-less tank and give them a mop or two.

Eggs are much easier to spot on a man-made mop as shown above. Not all eggs will stay well. If an egg goes bad, perhaps since it is infertile, it will turn milky. If left alone for a prolonged period, fungus will grow on milky eggs. Remove bad eggs as soon as you see them. The fungus or bacteria will spread quickly to healthy eggs nearby.

Healthy eggs, on the other hand, is totally transparent when newly fertilized, and get deeper in colour day after day. Eventually, the eggs will eye-up, i.e. when you can see clearly the head and eyes very well developed inside.

To pick the eggs, I use a pair of tweezers with a long and soft tip. Avoid touching them with our fingers as they may be oily or dirty. Rinse our hands with plenty of water before handling to get rid of the last bit of detergent. Put the eggs in a cup with water from the parent tank.

I will also put in some Java Moss. Java Moss helps to provide oxygen. In case a fry or two hatched too early without me knowing, they may feed themselves with micro-organisms on the Moss as a temporary relieve. Mark the species name and date of collection on the cup and put it away from direct light. Check the eggs daily so that bad ones could be removed and fry be isolated and fed.

I use light colour mop as well. In this case shown above, light blue. It seems that colour is not important.

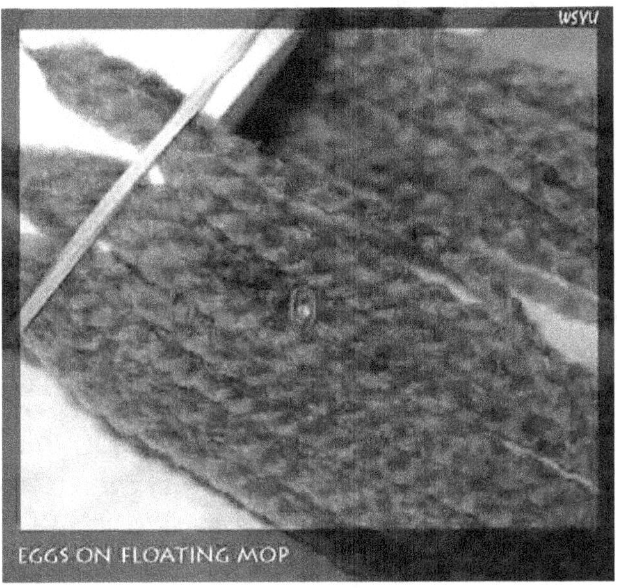

Mops are normally clipped onto one side of an aquarium for convenience. However, one may try floating the mop and let it drifts. The mop above is tied onto a piece of Styrofoam with a rubber band and let float freely. You can use whatever that works for you. Some people use corks. For me, I use the base of a Styrofoam cup.

Before putting the mop back in the water or before putting it away for storage, rinse and microwave the mop in hot water. Replace with new mops every month.

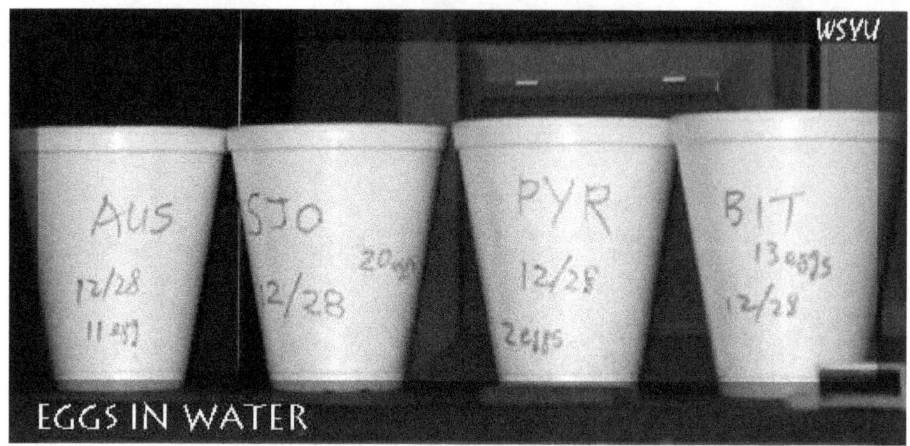

Egg collection date marking on the cups are just for reference. I will have to check each cup daily to remove bad eggs, and to remove and feed fry that somehow hatched early etc. On this particular day, I have less eggs from my AUS, BIT and PYR than usual. My pair of SJO, on the other hand, is doing quite a nice job. The next thing to do is to decide if I should give the eggs away, sell them, or hatch and keep them.

Incubation time for non-annuals is species specific. The shortest being just slightly over one week. If you want to delay their incubation, transfer and store them in moist peat moss. You will learn how to do that in a later section for Annuals. If you intend to sell your eggs, check your mops daily so that you can transfer them for storage in moist peat moss in the earliest possible time. You need as much time in selling your eggs as possible and you need to slow down their incubation. For details, refer to the section on selling eggs. On the other hand if you are hatching the eggs and raising the fry, check the mop twice a week and store them in a cup with water from the same tank.

4.3 Egg Collection for Annuals

Annuals like Nothobranchius like **RAC** above bury their eggs if they can do so. To collect their eggs, keep the base of the aquarium bare and give them a bowl of shallow peat moss for burying their eggs into.

Peat moss is the most common medium of all. It is not only used as the spawning medium, but also used as a storage medium. The slight acidity of peat moss is another reason that it is good as a storing medium. Another spawning medium that I use for Annuals is very fine and smooth sand. One can easily separate the eggs from the sand by sifting. Sand cannot be used as a storage medium as eggs may suffocate if stored for a prolonged period.

As described in section 2.5, dried peat moss should be boiled in water and let cooled so that they will sink. Fill up a small bowl with an inch high of peat moss, cover it up with a piece of plastic wrap, and lower the bowl into the tank very slowly. As soon as the bowl is completely filled with water, remove the wrap slowly. The wrap prevents peat moss from spreading all over the tank when we lower the bowl into the water. Below: the bowl was in place and the male was eager to check it out. In this case, I used a red bowl since it went well with my aquarium setup. Name of the fish: **Nothobranchius korthausae Yellow**, or simply **KOR Yellow**.

Annuals eggs have an average incubation time from 1 to 6 months. Once a week, we remove the bowl or cup of peat moss from the tank and place the wet peat moss between thick layers of newspaper for a few hours to dry most of the water out. The peat moss should look dry but feel moist to the touch. If touching the peat moss wet your finger in any way, it is too wet. Do not dry up everything. If it happens, quickly add some water back from the parent tank or else the eggs will die. You may want to sample the peat moss for sight of eggs or you may just put the peat moss away for storage without sampling. It could take a long time, say 15 minutes or more, for you to locate the first few eggs in the peat if you have no prior experience in doing so. Just be patient the first few times you are checking for eggs and your skills will improve very quickly after that.

Store the peat in a plastic bag and label it with the name of the fish and the date of collection. Don't squeeze every bit of air out of the bag as the eggs are alive inside. Place the bag in a cool and dark place, like in a closet. Check perhaps twice monthly to see if the peat is still moist. If not, add a few drops of water from your tank. When it is near the end of the incubation period, check also the development of the eggs by sampling. Incubation period varies according to species. It could be as short as 4 weeks or as long as several months.

When I need to count my eggs, I use sand as the spawning medium instead of peat moss. Sand for reptiles was all I could find at my local pet stores and so I used them. The sand must be fine enough for the sifting and smooth enough to be safe with the eggs. Unlike mops, they seems to prefer sand with a deeper colour. Sift the sand to remove larger grains, rinse until the water is no longer milky, and microwave them in hot water before using. After cooling down, put an inch of them in a bowl and lower the bowl into position in the tank. Sand is heavy and they won't fly all over the tank during the lowering of the bowl. A plastic wrap is not needed.

A bowl of sand was used in the photo above. Even though the tank has pebble substrate, they prefer sand to pebbles as they can bury their eggs in them. I remove the bowl twice a week for egg collection as I found them very prolific. Name of the fish: **Nothobranchius korthausae Red** or simply **KOR Red**.

Take the bowl out, transfer the sand with a spoon to a sieve and hope that you have eggs!

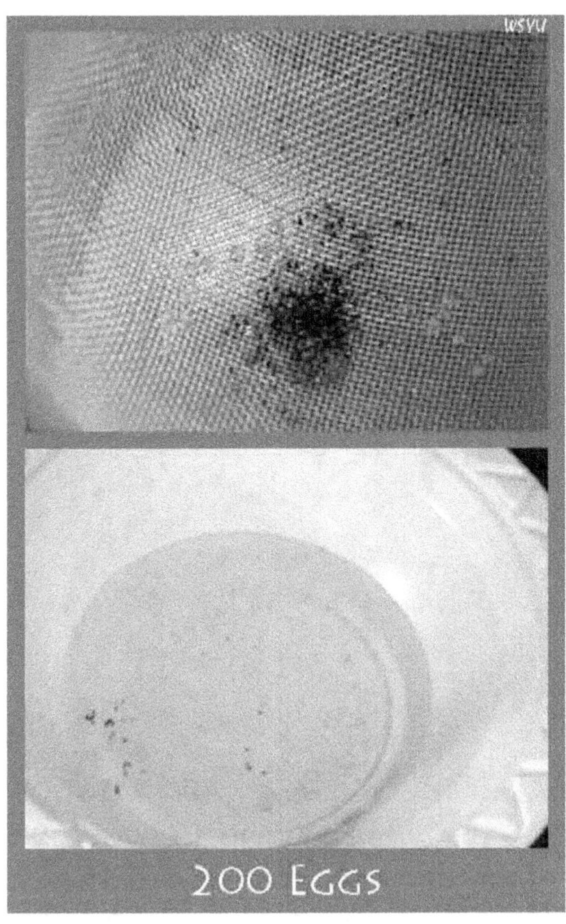

There they were! And there were around 200 eggs in that bowl of sand!

4.4 Egg Collection for Semi-Annuals

Semi-Annuals show characteristics midway between the annuals and non-annuals. Feel free to try mop and peat moss to see which spawning medium they prefer. These **SJO** shown above love to lay eggs anywhere at the bottom. I was trying to be lazy and collect their eggs with a blue nylon sheet. There was no luck. Eggs did not stick well to the sheet and they ate the eggs.

I tried using Sphagnum Moss, as shown above. Guess eggs didn't stick well to them either. But even if they did, the light yellowish colour would make egg picking very difficult.

A collection net made of yarn worked very well. In fact, simply put a long mop that extends long enough to cover part of the tank bottom would work very well as well. Experimenting different ways of doing things makes fish keeping a lot more interesting.

4.5 Egg Collection for Peat Divers

Annual Peat divers dive! We have to give them a spawning medium of at least 2 inches thick. Sand is too dense and heavy for the diving and peat moss is used.

Above: Like peat spawning annuals, we can keep as much plants in the tank as we like for peat divers.

Peat divers will be frustrated if they are not able to find a place to dive in. The **PCR** above is confused. The peat moss substrate there is too thin for him.

Above: PCR checking out his bowl of deep peat moss.

Knowing that he has a deep bowl of peat, this male **MAG** goes around and invites females to follow him back to the bowl. It will not be successful every time but he gets lucky. This time two females returned with him.

The male dips his head several times slightly into the peat while keeping an eye on the females. He wants to be sure that a female is committed.

The male submerged and a female followed immediately after. I have no idea how they could find each other but after a while, the male would leave by ejecting itself vertically out of the peat in a very high speed. A few moments later, the female would slowly emerge. She would take her time looking around before fully leaving the peat moss.

The following is a summary.

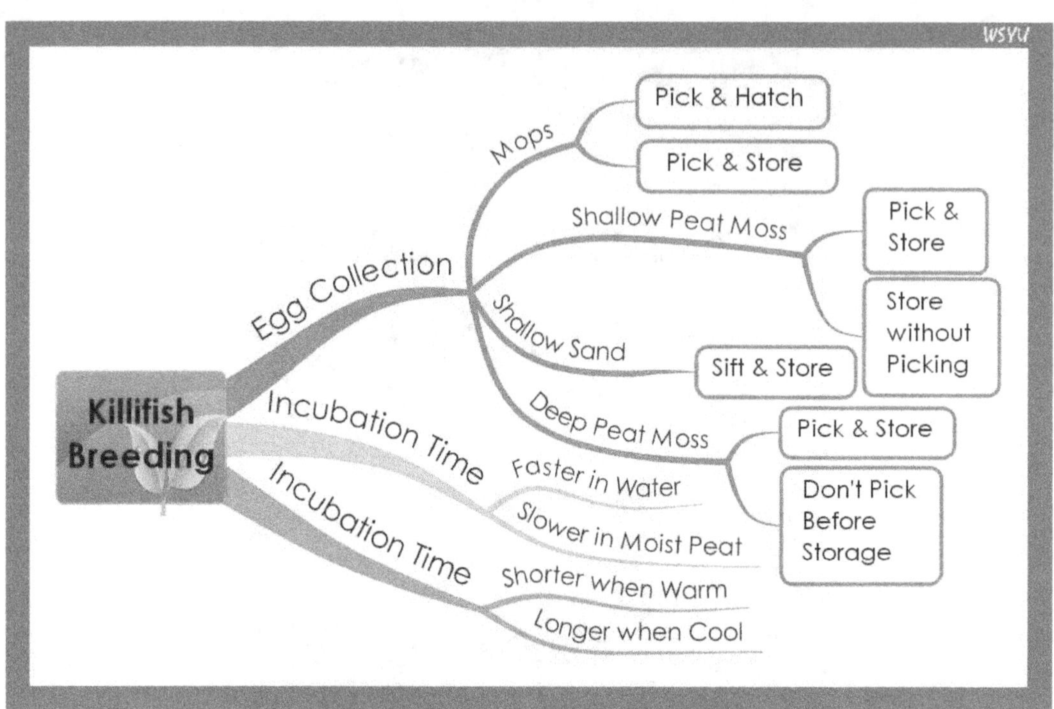

Killifish Breeding
Egg Collection
Mops
Pick & Hatch
Pick & Store
Shallow Peat Moss
Pick & Store
Store without Picking
Shallow Sand
Sift & Store
Deep Peat Moss
Pick & Store
Don't Pick Before Storage
Incubation Time
Faster in Water
Slower in Moist Peat
Incubation Time
Shorter when Warm
Longer when Cool

4.6 Hatching Eggs of Non-Annuals and Semi-Annuals

Eggs collected previously

Water quality in a cup remains pretty much the same unless one or more eggs went bad. Check every cup of eggs daily and remove the bad ones. Replenish water from the tank if necessary. The colour of the good ones will deepen day after day. Put the cup away from direct lighting again after the checking.

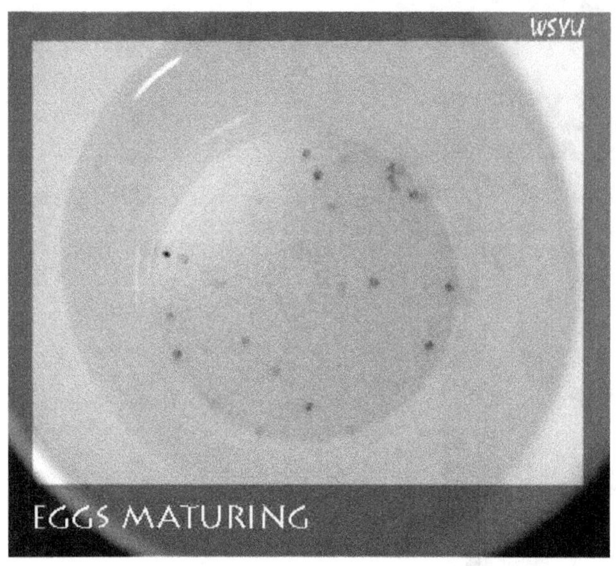

Development is in good progress and their eyes are showing up in just a few days. Some eggs mature faster than others.

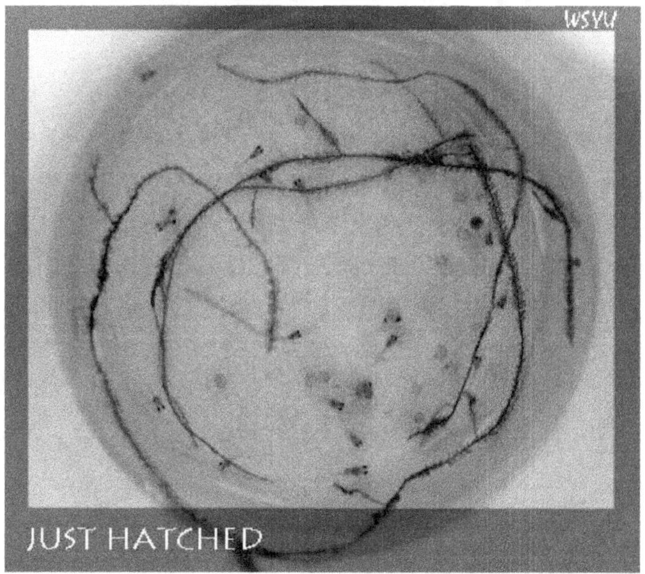

Above: most eggs are hatched in the same day, leaving the remain of egg shells behind. Use a large dropper to move the fry to a small container for water matching. If all are hatched, it is OK to do water matching right in the cup and pour the contents into their rearing tank all at once after the water matching is done. Remember, match both the water qualities and temperature.

Keep the water level in the rearing tank low at the beginning, about an inch or two to start with for ease of feeding and removal of excess food. Use live vinegar eels first. When they grow bigger and start to ignore the vinegar eels, switch to live baby brine shrimps. They will ignore baby brine shrimps once they get still bigger. Feed them with frozen brine shrimps or live adult brine shrimps or Grindal worms. Live foods for fry are very easy to culture at home and they are covered here in section 7.1.

Eggs in a tank

If the eggs are hard to come by or very expensive, you may want to give them more water and oxygen, like putting them in a tank with an inch or two of water. Shallow water has a larger oxygen contents as the total surface area in contact with the atmosphere is a constant no matter how deep the water is. Greater distance between eggs in a tank will also minimize the hazard of fungus spreading from a bad egg. To supply even more oxygen, use an air stone and air pump.

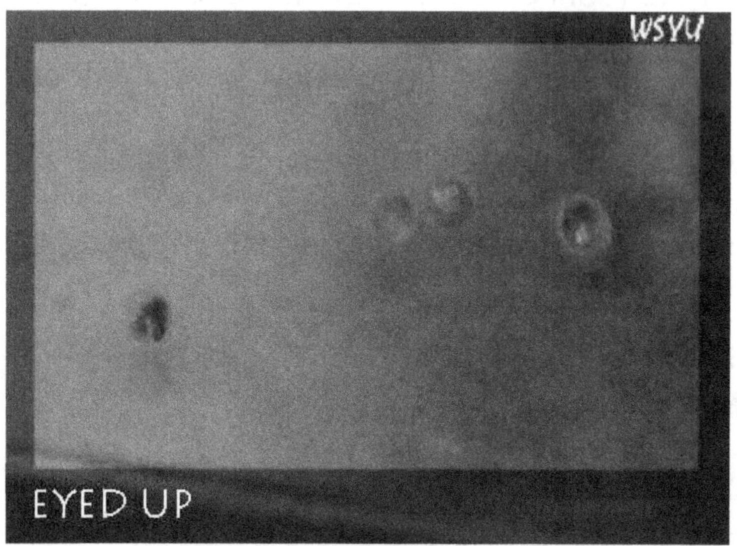

Eggs have eyed-up.

One can see more clearly in the close-up above that the eggs have now **eyed-up**. Some species show golden iris when eyed-up but some do not. These eggs might hatch any time now. Unfortunately, not all eyed-up eggs will hatch. Breeders and hobbyists have tried many ways to force hatch stubborn eyed-up eggs but so far, there is no sure way of doing so. One popular way is to put such stubborn eggs and water into a small container; blow air and thus carbon dioxide with your month into the container and put the cap on; put the container in your pant pocket and start walking around. Hopefully, such warm up and shaking would "wake" the "fry" up and break the egg shells.

4.7 Hatching Eggs of Annuals and Peat Divers

As discussed earlier, eggs of annuals and peat-divers are stored in moist peat moss. Check the peat with a tweezers for eyed-up eggs a few days before the recommended time of incubation is up. The recommended incubation time may have already been provided to you by the seller. If not, check species specific information online.

Since it would be time consuming to look for every egg in a pile of moist peat moss, we will only do a quick sampling. If the incubation time has passed but not too many eggs that I could find are eyed-up, wait and check again in a week. A cooler temperature or a dryer storage medium will slow down the egg development process. If many eggs have eyed-up, wet the peat with water from the tank that will house the fry.

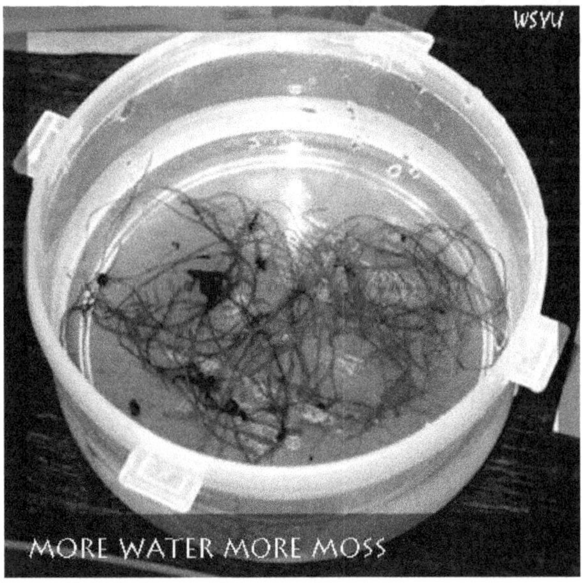

Bigger container for more water

The above is my hatching container with water and Java Moss. It is bigger than those Styrofoam cups that I use for non-annuals since I will be putting the egg storage medium of peat moss into it as well. Make sure that the water is shallow enough for a good oxygen content. It is now time to put the eggs and peat moss in and put the container away from direct light. Come back and check every couple hour to see if they are hatched.

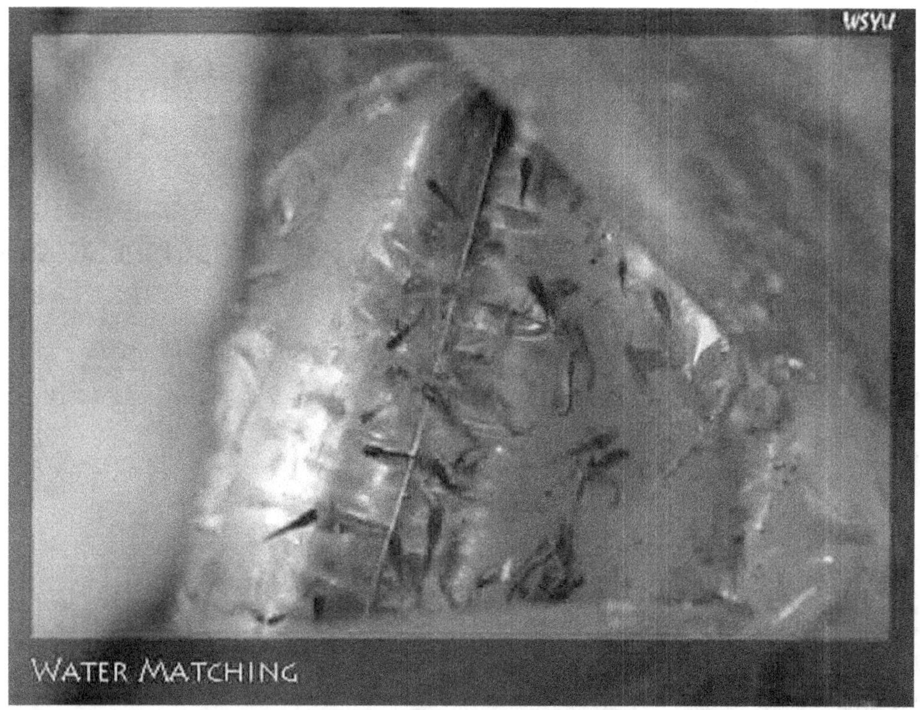

As above, do a water matching of water temperature and qualities as described in section 3.4 before releasing newly hatched fry into their tank.

Eggs collected on the same day and stored in the same bag of peat moss may develop in different paces. If you are not sure that most or all eggs have hatched. Dry the peat moss again and put it away for 2 weeks. Repeat the checking and re-wet of the peat moss.

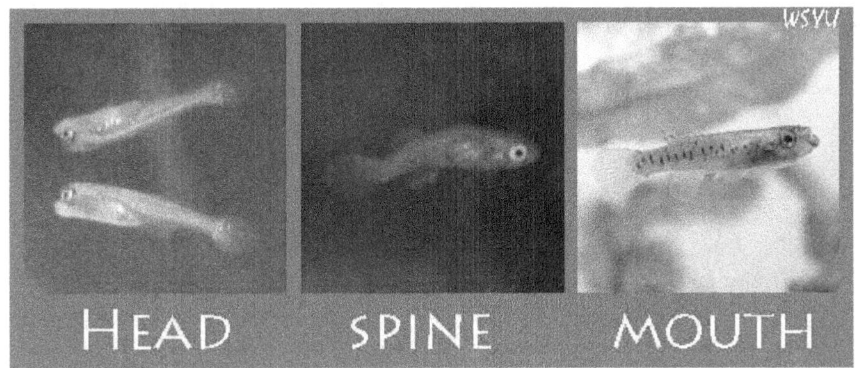

Unfortunately, hatched fry may have defects, though not too often. I have registered several kinds; belly sliding is the most common; curved spine is next. Other defects shown above are rarely seen; the one on the right has a normally open mouth while the one on the left is half-headed. I have strong feelings for this half-head. It was a KOR Red, the eggs of which was relatively hard to get back in 2005. It was incapable of taking food in; yet it swam around the tank and examined every inch in a rather graceful manner. It died a day or two later. Guess it wanted to stay and it was sad.

4.8 Rearing Fry

DIAPTERON GEORGIAE FRIES

Fry won't jump. There is no need to put a lid on. For their rearing tank, instead of using a full tank of water and doing partial water change, we start with about one inch deep of water. Add clean conditioned water of half an inch every two day until the tank is 80% full. This will be a lot easier than doing partial water changes.

With a smaller water volume, the fry will have an easier time finding their live foods. Also, we ourselves will have an easier time removing excess food or possibly, dead fry. Do not feed more food than necessary as excess vinegar eels and baby brine shrimps will die in fresh water in an hour or two and foul the water.

So how much food is enough? When feeding fry, add a little bit, wait, check if most food are consumed, then add a little bit more. Wait longer if you have only a few fry or if the tank is bigger as the fry will take longer to locate their food.

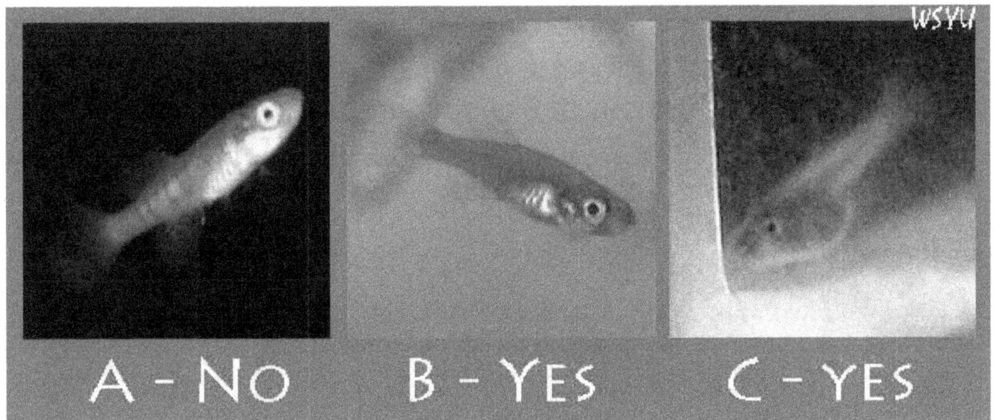

Above: Fry A on the left, is starving. Fry B looks good, if it is already an hour or two after the last feeding. Fry C with a full belly on the right looks good if that is right after the feeding. Don't feed any more when most fry have a big belly like that of fry C. If you suspect that you have over-fed, remove excess food (and other debris) immediately with a dropper.

As shown above, some fry grow a lot faster than others. This is especially true with some males. Separate the big ones from time to time to speed up the growth of the smaller ones. (The blue wires on the right, by the way, are DC lines driving the DIY cooling fans and LED lighting.) Fish in the tank: **PCR**.

Alternately, remove the smaller ones if they are the minority. Since egg-storing medium peat moss was put into the tank together with the eggs for hatching, the water looked less clear. Fish in the tank: **RAC**.

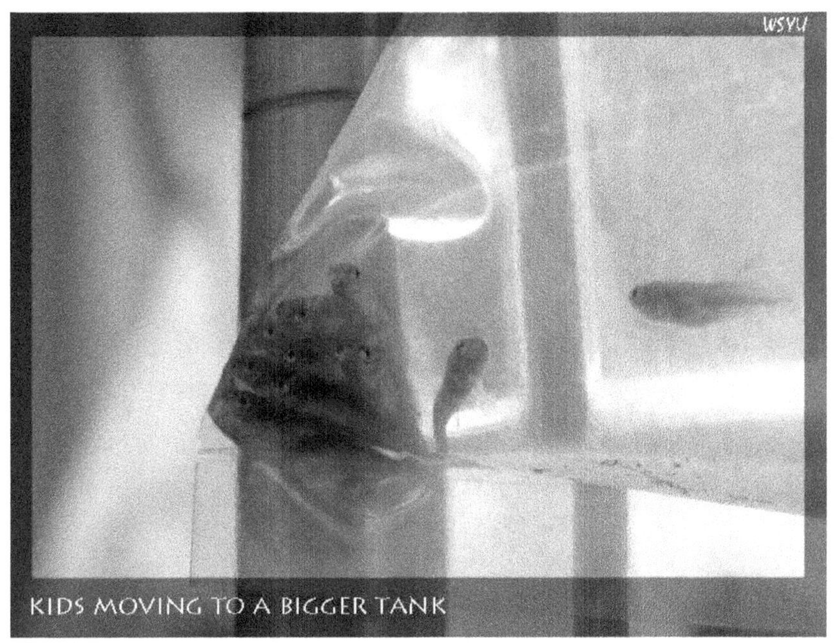

Doing water matching again for these 20 mm long kids before putting them into a bigger setup. Name of killie: **Aphyosemion ogoense GHP 80-24**.

These bigger kids would stay in their new home until fully mature.

Yet Bigger Now.

Big enough for the studio tank and ready for spawning!

Hatching eggs and watching them growing up is a great joy in fish keeping!

Growing up - **BIT** (Left) and **FOE** (Right)

Growing Up - **ELB** (Left) and **SJO** (Right)

4.9 Hatching Diary of Nothobranchius furzeri MZM 04-3

FUR has a short lifespan of 4 months or so. If you want to observe the whole life cycle of a fish in a short period of time, FUR may be right for you. However, since they grow very rapidly, **you have to feed them much more often than other species**, say four times a day.

Getting the hatching tank ready

Since FUR is a little more expensive and is not always easy to come by, I use a hatching tank instead of a small container. I keep the water level low for a better oxygen exchange with the atmosphere, use an air-stone, and put in a driftwood with Java Moss. Driftwood is not necessary but as Java Moss was tied onto one of my driftwood, I put it in. The setup was prepared well before the eggs are ready to be wetted. Some planning is always good in keeping killies especially if you want to deal with eggs and fry.

Day 0 - Eggs in the tank

I purchased 30 eggs. Not sure if the seller has given me a few more as a safety measure or not and I found one dozen in the moist peat. It is hard to find every single egg in a pile of peat moss. Also, not all eggs will mature and some will just perish and gone in their storage medium. Out of all the eggs that I could find, six are eyed-up. I put these eyed-up eggs and half of the peat moss into the hatching tank and wait.

Day 1 - All six eggs were hatched overnight but all I could see was four fry. The other two were never found.

Day 5 - Fry were still very small and had not growth much. Only three of them were captured in the photo.

Day 7 - Still very small but looked quite alright, judging from its belly after feeding.

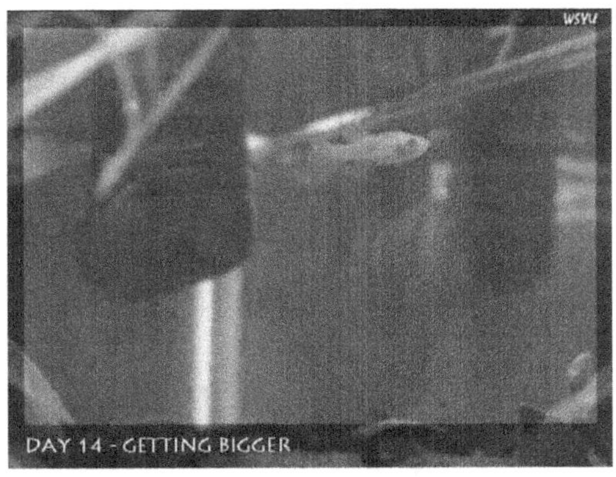

Day 14 - The two females were smaller in size.

Day 18 - Males were a lot bigger. Colour was just starting to show.

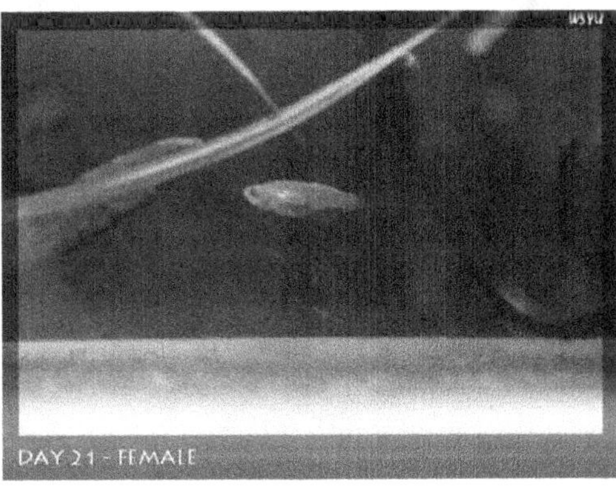

Day 21 - Females were still quite small.

Day 24 - Females were bigger now but still a lot smaller than the males.

Day 26 - The two males were put in two separate tanks.

Day 30 - A rough measurement was taken. It was more colourful than just 4 days ago.

Day 32 - It was like a quantum growth in just 2 days!

Day 34 - Still bigger!

Day 41 - Fully matured!

Day 41 - Both of them!

4.10 Genetic Degradation

If we start off breeding with one pair of killifish, we would have several generations of them in our home in just one year. If we keep on breeding without introducing new gene diversity, perhaps by buying eggs or fish of the same species from a good breeder and mix them in the family, the problem of genetic degradation will start to become apparent. You will start to see a fade in colour and then later on even a change of body shape for the worse.

As mentioned before, egg or fish names ending with F1 or F2 are respectively the first and second generation offspring of a wild-catch fish. They are very desirable for breeding purposes. Breeding killifish or any fish in a genetical meaningful way is always a challenge for fish breeders.

End of Chapter Four

WSYW
APHYOSEMION ELBERTI N'TUI

WSYU
NOTHOBRANCHIUS PATRIZII

Chapter 5. Setup Enhancements

5.0 Introduction

This chapter describes enhancements that could be fun to implement. Such enhancements are NOT a must in keeping and breeding killifish. However, since finding new ways of doing things is part of the fun in fish keeping, I encourage you to try them out and improvise in any way you like. As long as you keep the temperature and water quality stable, you will be doing just fine.

5.1 Semi-automatic Water Change

One may consider using some kind of automatic water change to lessen the time one spends in the maintenance of their aquariums. A fully automatic system will mean a system that does all the water change automatically. Perhaps a timer is used to trigger a small partial water change daily, or perhaps fresh conditioned water is introduced continuously 24 hours a day using water drippers for gardening. An overflow is made available in each of the tank so that aged water is continuously pushed out of the tank with the introduction of fresh conditioned water.

A simpler way is to use a semi-automatic water change system with just the overflow system instead. Water is added manually by pulling a Vinyl hose and turning on a tap from water storage tanks located near the ceiling. The time and trouble doing water changes is greatly reduced.

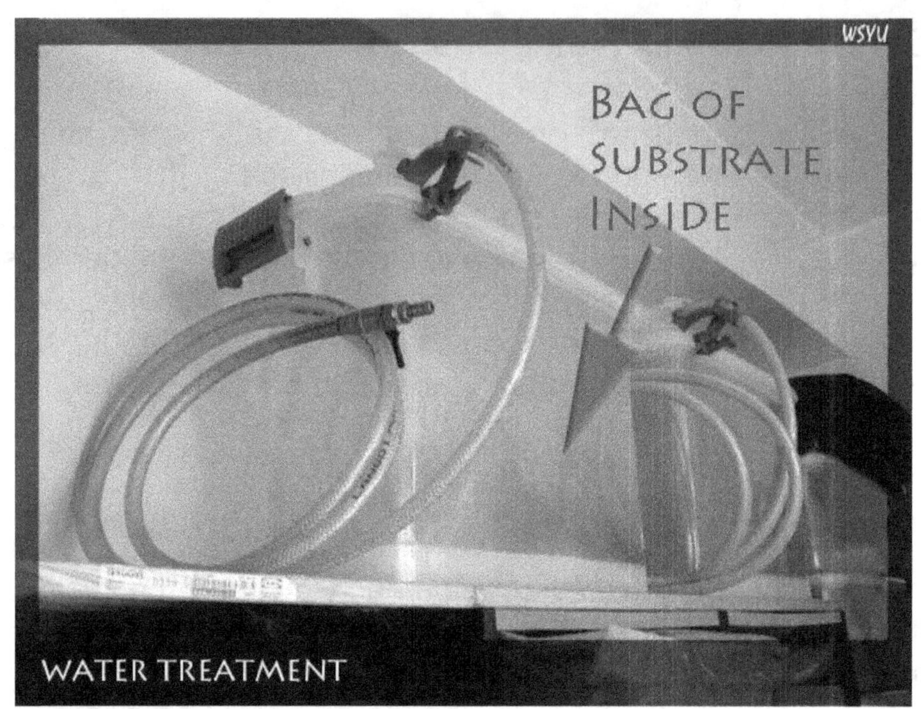

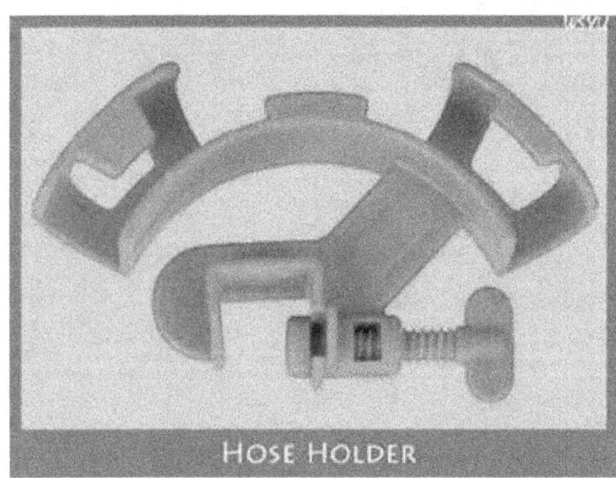

Hose holder can be purchased online.

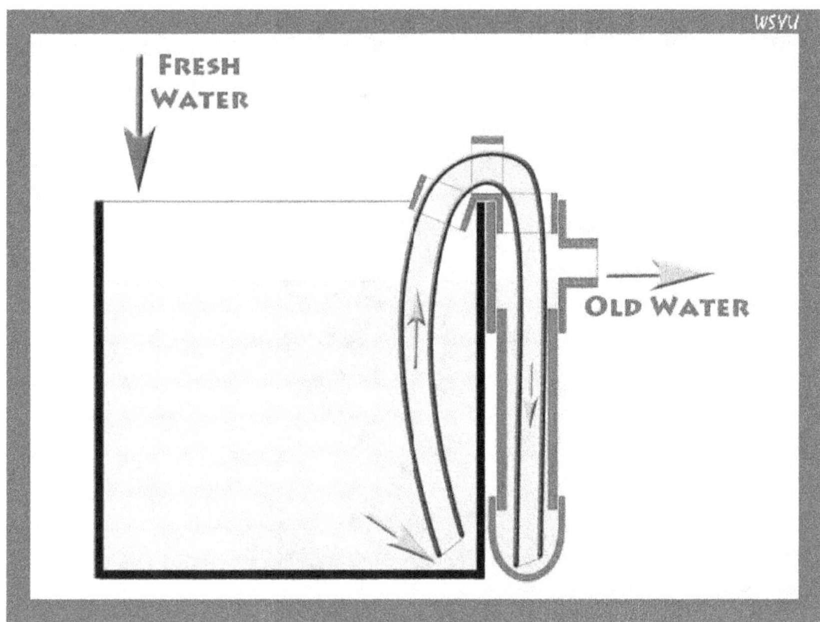

Old water at the bottom get pushed out to the draining tube when fresh new water is added.

There are two types of water overflow. External hook-up or drill-through-the-glass type. I do not want to drill through my tanks and I designed my own external overflow unit.

The external unit is just an extension of the tank if a continuous water column could be kept in the tube that links the tank and the external unit together. Atmospheric pressure will keep water level the same inside and out. Instead of drilling a hole in the tank at the desired water level, I provide an outlet at the external hook-up.

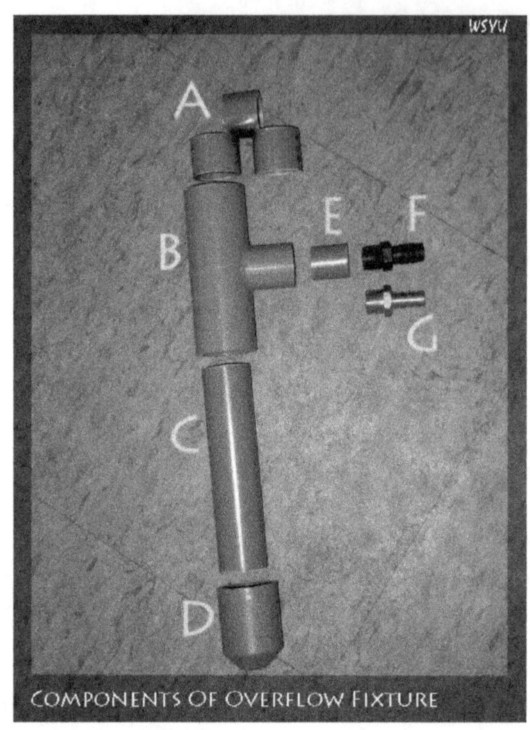

The above shows my design of an overflow unit. I use inexpensive PVC pipes. Since I could find parts A to E with tight tolerance, there is no need to seal the parts together with glue. All I need is to press fit the parts together. If you do not find parts with matching tolerance, seal the assembly with glue. Part G is a metal nozzle while part F is a more expensive plastic version. Use whatever is easily available to you. The nozzle is to be secured to the draining tube discussed below.

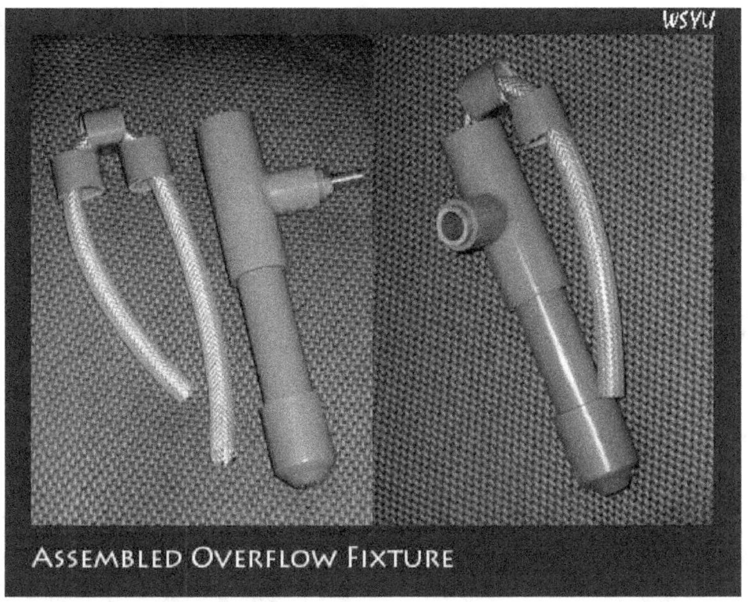

The parts are assembled as shown above. The metal nozzle would be permanently secured to the drain tube discussed below instead. The deeper your tank, the longer is the transparent Vinyl tube as you want its opening to stay close to the bottom of the tank. There is no need to make the external PVC fixture longer for deeper tanks.

Drain tubes fit with nozzles are tied to the rack. Just enough tape was wound around the nozzle so that the nozzle could be slid easily by hand into and out of the overflow fixture without water leak.

Drain tubes from all the tanks go into a collection pipe hanging at the very bottom of the rack.

To complete the installation:

1. Dip an assembled overflow fixture completely into the water in the tank.

2. Wait until both the PVC fixture and the Vinyl tube inside the fixture is fully filled with water.

3. Move the unit close to the back side near the surface, seal the end of the transparent Vinyl tube with your thumb and quickly lift and hang the fixture on the back pane of the tank so that the Vinyl

tube is still filled COMPLETELY with water. This may have to be attempted several times until you get the hang of it.

4. Slip the drain tube nozzle into the fixture.

Water in the tank will remain level with the drain tube position. When fresh water is introduced, old water near the Vinyl tube opening at the bottom of the tank is pushed out. You should test if it works by adding conditioned water into the tank immediately after the installation. Water in the tank exceeding the drain tube level will flow out of the tank SLOWLY. If the flow does not start, the Vinyl tube is probably not completely filled with water.

5.2 Oxygen Enhancement

A good supply of oxygen is important for fish. This is especially true in summer time when the water temperature is high and oxygen dissolves less in water. To increase oxygen content other than lowering the water temperature, we may turn the air pump volume up. However, too much turbulence could tire the fish out very quickly.

One way of increasing the oxygen content is by running the water against porous lava rocks along a tube, as shown below. Oxygen is blend into the water along the way. The longer the tube with rocks, the better is the results. For my one foot tanks, the tube is short. However, the difference is measurable using commercial oxygen test kits.

Two tanks were set up above at the same time for my oxygen test. Same amount of water from the same water source. Just about an equal amount of plants are put in as well to mimic most of my other tanks. Finally, I make sure that similar amount of air flow are provided to each filter before attaching a tube of lava rocks to one of the filter outputs.

There is an oxygen increase of 1/3 after an hour of running water through the tube of lava rocks when checked by an oxygen test kit! Not too scientific and perhaps not conclusive but I feel good about the setup.

5.3 Tank Management

Smaller tanks are more flexible for my purpose of breeding killifish. On the right hand side of the photo, there is a column of yet smaller 6-inch tanks for egg hatching and fry rearing.

Putting new tanks up on the shelf. Note the overflow fixtures to be installed, two water storage bins on the floor, and a battery operated siphon with a red cap and on/off button. Obviously, one need to get things organized when you have many tanks and fish, and many packages of eggs in the closet.

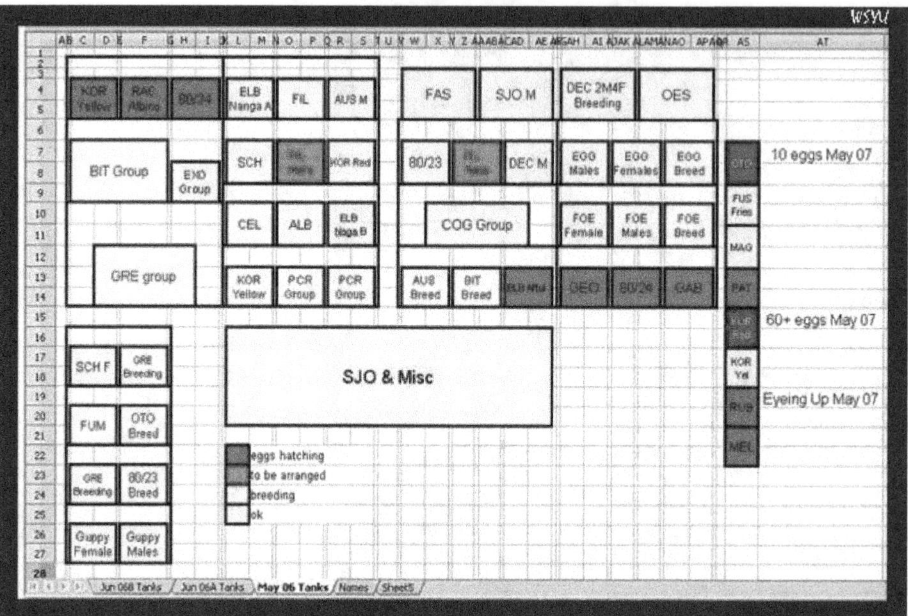

I use Excel to keep track of all my tanks, fish, and eggs with their collection and expected hatching dates. The relative sizes of my tanks are also roughly shown to make my planning easy. One may use OpenOffice instead of Excel as it is a very capable freeware.

End of Chapter Five

NOTHOBRANCHIUS RUBRIPINNIS TZ83 ALBINO

NOTHOBRANCHIUS KORTHAUSAE RED

Chapter 6. Buying and Selling Eggs

6.1 Buying Eggs

One convenient way of acquiring the killifish that you like is by buying or bidding eggs online. The supply of killifish eggs is much more abundant nowadays than just a few years ago. Price is getting cheaper as well. As with all other online transactions, do not pay cash or use cash-equivalent payment methods. Also do not disclose your credit card information to the sellers. Use services like PayPal.

As with live fish, each seller has his or her own way of packaging eggs. The following is an example of what I did with the eggs that I once bought.

It was the first time that I bought from this seller and I was curious to find out how he would do the packaging. The box that I received was big for 30 eggs!

It was very well packed! The species name was labelled on the sealed package inside.

Unsealed the package and there they were! The eggs in peat moss were stored in a small plastic container with a label stating the species name, eggs collection date and recommended hatching date or the date that you may wet the eggs. It was very nicely done! There is a free gift of food in a plastic bag too!

It is very important that one samples the eggs immediately after receiving the package. If anything goes wrong, for instance, in case of not finding a single egg or finding too many bad eggs, the buyer has to report it to the seller immediately for a claim. To be fair, a small percentage of healthy looking eggs could perish and completely vanish during the journey. The total number of eggs that arrived safely may be slightly less than the number that you purchased. Some sellers will put a few more eggs just in case but some will not. Apart from estimating if enough eggs are there, the buyer should examine how well developed the eggs are. If some are very well developed, prepare for the hatching. Do not rely on the hatching date provided by the seller.

For those buyers experienced with picking eggs, if the pile of peat moss is small and manageable, they may check every bit of the peat moss for eggs as they can do so rather quickly. However, if the seller put the eggs in a big bag of peat moss for reasons that I still do not understand, even the experienced can only do guess work on the number of eggs and on the stage of egg development based on the first few eggs found.

For beginners, if the pile of peat moss is small and manageable, they will very likely attempt to find every single egg. However, beginners may have difficulty spotting the eggs. The number of eggs found could be a lot less than the actual number of eggs in the peat moss.

In this example, the amount of peat moss arrived this time was just about right and manageable. I therefore decided to examine everything. I used a sheet of light reflecting aluminium foil as my working surface as it made my egg finding a lot easier.

Some of the eggs matured a lot faster than expected. After a few minutes of checking, I put all eyed-up eggs in one bottle and the rest in another with their original peat moss. I decided to wet the eyed-up eggs a few days later when their hatching and rearing tanks were ready. As per the other bottle of eggs that were not yet mature, I labelled it with the species name, number of eggs, and the date that I have examined them. I would examine the eggs again in another 2 weeks.

The hatching date provided by the seller is for reference only. Not only factors like temperature and moisture might affect the speed of egg development, eggs collected on the same day and stored in the same bag of peat moss may also develop in different paces. Unless you know that the eggs have eyed-up for a long time, there is no immediate need to wet them just because the incubation time is up. If you are busy with something else or if your hatching setup is not yet ready, defer the wetting. Egg hatching has been discussed in section 4.7.

6.2 Selling Your Eggs

There are times when you have way too many eggs than you can hatch or even give away. In that case, sell them! The money I received by selling 2 packs of eggs (12 plus eggs for Non-Annuals and 30 plus eggs for Annuals per pack is the norm) a week has covered most of my expenses in running an air-conditioned fish room in my house! Just make sure that you have some not too common species on offer. (Again, not too common species are not necessarily harder to keep and breed. All you need to do is follow my advices in this book.)

First of all, this is apparently a sales task. It would help if you could post a nice photo of the parent fish. If your photo look nicer than those of other sellers, you will be at an absolute advantage. I managed to charge 50% more than my competitors for exactly the same species simply because my photos looked much better. The process of photographing fish is described in Chapter 8. Of course at the end, the customer paying 50% more need to receive a professionally packed eggs with high hatching rate before he could leave you a 5-star review. More on that later.

Second of all, customer focus is importance. I was the first seller, as far as I know, who posted images of the parents in two lighting conditions: with and without using flash light. Fish exhibits different colours in the photo under different lighting conditions. The buyer would be disappointed if the fish grow up to something different from his or her expectation.

The above is an example of the photos that I posted in my selling descriptions. Notice how colourful the flashed image on the right looks.

80-23 looks nice with or without camera flash but taste is certainly personal.

Well, a customer has just transferred his money to you by PayPal! It is time to pack the eggs up nicely! Before I continue, I must say that it is not a good thing trying to sell eggs that you do not yet have. Your fish, say several productive pairs of the same kind, may all of a sudden all stop laying eggs for no apparent reason for many days to come. Keeping your customer waiting is a terrible thing in sales. To slow down the development of eggs of non-annuals while you wait for a customer order, store the eggs in moist peat moss.

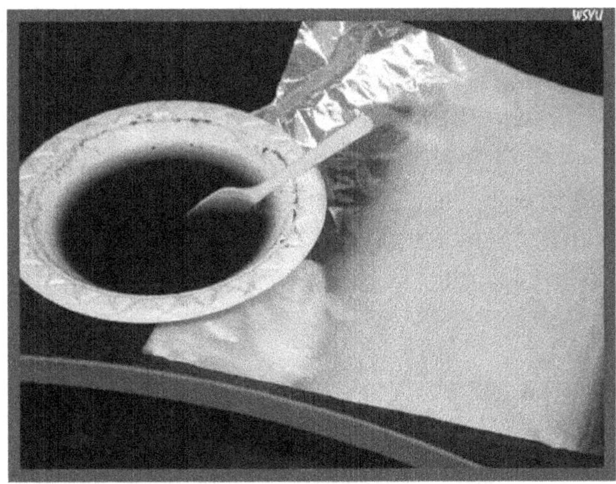

A. Get a bowl of microwaved and now cooled peat moss ready, subdue the light and use a new piece of aluminium foil as the working surface. The following process is my way of packing eggs. You do not have to pack them the same way I did. Just improvise! The advantages of my method will be explained later.

B. Scoop peat moss out of the bowl and arrange them to form two rectangles with a thickness of 3-mm or one eighth of an inch. Try to scoop as little water out of the bowl as possible. Size of the rectangle is obviously dependable on the number of eggs that you sold. They are about 1x1.5-inch or 3x4-cm long for storing 15 eggs.

C. Pick the eggs up one by one with a tweezers and put them on top of one peat rectangle. Even out the distance between eggs. For me, I will always put more eggs than advertised just in case that some go bad. Most of the time, the eggs were all good after the journey and customers were delighted with the extra. By the way, if eggs really went bad after the journey, resend eggs. I did so on my own expense while some sellers may charge another round of "freight and handling".

D. Cover the eggs up with the other peat rectangle. It would be tough to transfer a whole rectangle at a time. Transfer just one slice at a time, as shown above.

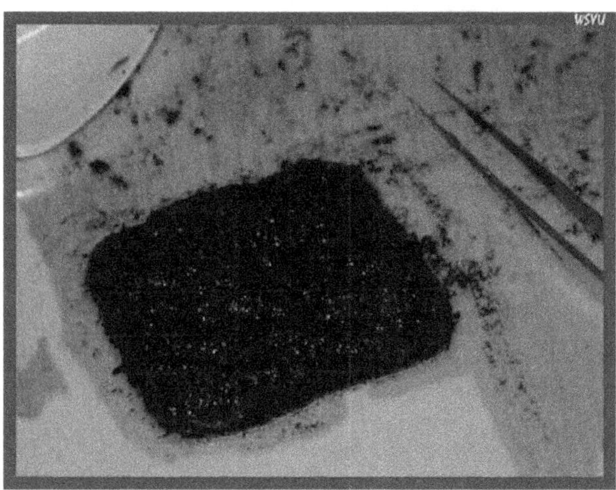

The stacking was done!

E. Remove excessive water from the peat moss with paper tissue. I will repeat the process until no more water can be picked up by a new piece of tissue. I can actually pick the "peat moss cake" up with my fingers now without breaking it up or wetting my fingers.

F. The peat moss cake holds up quite well since it is moist and not wet. Lift and put it in a zipper bag that is already marked with the full name of the species, number of eggs, and date of egg collection.

G. This bag of eggs will be put inside a slightly larger zipper bag, double seal with tape, and secure it in a very well padded envelope for the mailing. You will need to use express mail service for non-annual eggs as they have a short incubation period. For annual eggs, use the least expensive registered mail service that you can find.

There are two advantages packing the eggs the way I do. First, the package is small and either you save your customer on the shipping if you charge actual or you earn more out of the shipping if you charge a fixed amount. Second, my customer can simply ply the two layers of peat cake apart and count the eggs without the need of sorting through a pile of peat moss.

Unexpected things did happen. The mail got lost, the custom office of the buyer's country rejected the package, eggs gone bad on arrival, or eggs in our possession somehow gone bad and you don't have enough good eggs to send. The list goes on. The key to keep your customers happy upon tough times is to provide them with great customer service.

Great customer service can often be achieved by doing two simple things. First is to promptly advise your customer and let them know that they are being taken care of. Second is to let customer take charge. Provide them with options and let them be the ones who make the decision. Examples:

- I am sorry to hear that the eggs have gone bad/ the package was damaged. Would you prefer a full refund or should I send you again by Express Mail at no extra cost to you?

- I am sorry to hear that the eggs have gone bad/ the package was damaged. Would you prefer a full refund? Since I don't have eggs of the same species at this moment, would you prefer to wait for another collection or to get my eggs of SPECIES-NAME now instead at no extra cost? SPECIES-NAME is another beautiful species that I keep. Please check a photo of them as attached.

And you guessed right, I received nothing but 5-star reviews!

Last but certainly not least, refrain from competing with whom you bought your eggs or fish from. List your items for sale at some other times or in another platform.

End of Chapter Six

SIMPSONICTHYS PICTURATUS

WSYU
NEMATOLEBIAS PAPILLIFEROUS

Chapter 7. Foods

7.1 Food Self-Cultured For Fry

Killie fry take only live foods. Fortunately, culturing live food is easy. Soon after fry are hatched, feed them with vinegar eels. They will start ignoring vinegar eels when they get bigger at about a week or two old. At that time, we start feeding them with newly hatched baby brine shrimp.

Vinegar eels are very tiny worm like creatures of about 1-mm long. Buy one starter culture, i.e. one small portion of vinegar eels, online and one bottle of cider vinegar from your supermarket. Dilute the vinegar with an equal amount of water and store them in two separate bottles. As always, we want to have a backup bottle. Puncture each cap with a fine hole for the air to get in. Put in each bottle one eighth of an apple and half of the starter culture. Put them in a cool and dim place and wait for a week or two to see them multiply. No need of maintenance or feeding and this bottle of live eels will be good for at least a year if kept cool.

To feed them to your fry, siphon them out with a small dropper into a small paper coffee filter, rinse them slightly with a little bit of fresh water, reverse the filter and dip it into the fry container. Do not over feed. If you are not sure, dip the reversed filter into a cup of clean water before siphoning the vinegar eels and water into the fry container. Fry will stop eating vinegar eels when they grow bigger. This is the time to feed them with baby brine shrimps.

The following is my **baby brine shrimp** hatchery.

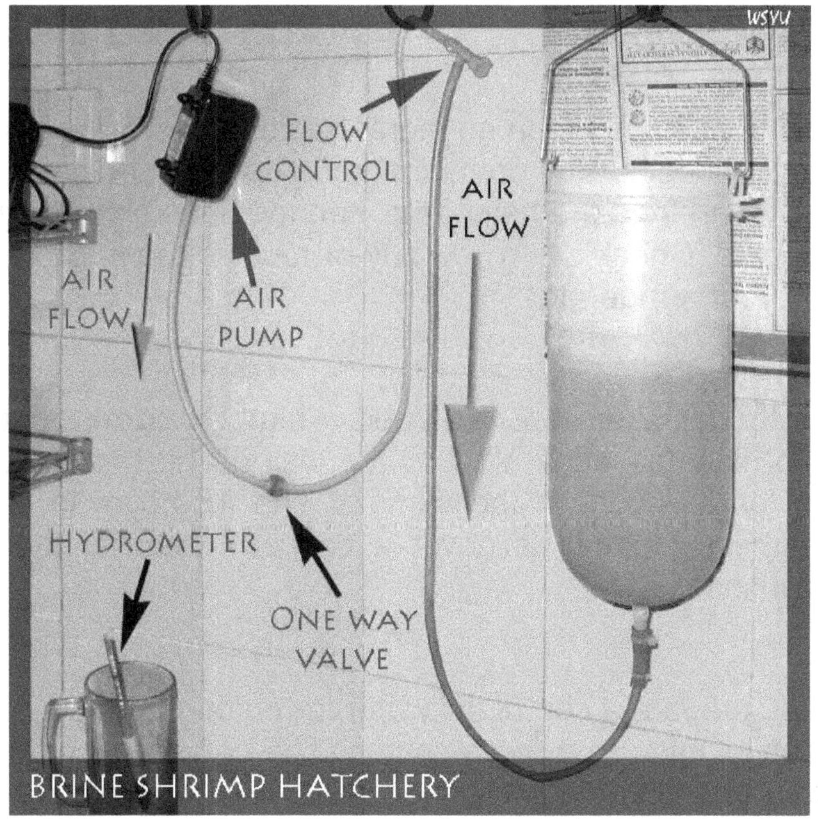

My brine shrimp hatchery shown above is relatively large due to the many fish that I keep. If you don't want to buy a commercially available brine shrimp hatcher, you can DIY one with a small 750 ml size soda bottle. Just cut the bottom, put a hole in the cap and glue an air tube in and hang the bottle upside down.

Brine shrimps live in salt water and you will need a floating **hydrometer** for measuring water salinity. Half fill the inverted bottle with tap water. Add a little salt from your kitchen, or use the cheapest kind of salt that you could buy, and turn the air pump on for one minute or until the salt dissolved. Turn the air pump off and measure with a hydrometer. Add more salt and repeat this step if it is needed until the hydrometer is floating on the marking that indicates the salinity of sea water.

For your first attempt, put in no more than one quarter of a teaspoon of brine shrimp eggs. Buy premium grade eggs as the hatch rate will be higher. Apart from the hatch rate, canned brine shrimp eggs have an expiry date. Check when you buy or receive them. Store the rest air tight in your refrigerator.

Now turn the air pump on. We need a high air current but not too high as to blow the eggs all over the wall of the bottle. Leave the pump on for 24 hours in the summer and 48 hours in the winter before harvest. Lighting is never a concern. Leaving them in the dark is just fine.

To harvest, prepare a cup of saltwater for putting the new born brine shrimp babies into. Stop the air pump. The babies will now move to the bottom of the bottle while their shells and the unhatched eggs will float to the surface.

Wait a minute or more. Unplug the end of the air tube near the air control. With the opening pinched, lower the air tube to point it to a very fine net, release and drain the liquid and babies. The babies will now be trapped in the net. Do not drain everything in the bottle as the top part is full of egg shells and unhatched eggs. Stop the flow to the net when there is about one inch of liquid left in the bottle.

Reverse the net and dip the baby brine shrimps into the cup of freshly made saltwater. Store them in the refrigerator and they will be good and alive for 2-3 days. Feed them to the fry as needed with a dropper. Since the amount needed is small, I feed them directly to the fry without rinsing them with fresh water.

Adjust the amount of water and brine shrimp eggs according to your needs. Normally, a pound of premium brine shrimp eggs will last a whole year for the average killie keepers and breeders. If you have no need to feed killie fry routinely and need only occasionally a very small amount of baby brine shrimps, there is no need for a brine shrimp hatchery. In this case, simply put some brine shrimp eggs in a shallow tray of salt water and wait for the hatch. Since there is no aeration, expect a longer time of hatching.

For fry, feeding 2 times a day is ok and feeding 3-4 times a day is good. Feeding only once daily however is not recommended as the fry may not be able to grow up fully to their proper size. Feeding fry has been covered with more detail in section 4.8. If you plan on going away for a long trip, delay hatching your killie eggs until you are back.

7.2 Food Purchased For Adults

Most killies take only frozen or live foods but not dry foods. Some killies on the other hand take only live foods. Fortunately, some live foods that killies love are not difficult to culture in our own homes. Before doing that, we will look around and see what is available for purchasing.

If you are lucky, you could find local suppliers that sell live adult brine shrimps as shown above. They have a lifespan of 3 days if kept in the refrigerator. If not, buy frozen brine shrimps as shown below.

Just break one cube and put it in a cup of water. You can start feeding when the cube starts melting and falling apart. You rinse them in the cup on the way of picking them up with a pair of tweezers. Just do not feed too much at a time. Add more only when everything in the tank is eaten. When their bellies are full or when they slow down the eating, stop feeding. Dispose the brine shrimp in the cup and use a fresh frozen cube every time.

I tried feeding them the shrimps that we eat and they loved them like crazy. I should have cut them into smaller pieces before feeding!

FUNDULOPANCHAX SJOESTEDTI DWARF BLUE VAKA

He was happy immediately after!

For adult killies, feeding 2 times a day is good, 3-4 times a day is great, and only once daily only if you are extremely busy. Feed very slowly and remove all leftover food a few minutes after the feeding. If you will be going away on a vacation or a business trip for a few days, turn off the light timer so that they are in as dark an environment as possible all the time until you come back. Darkness will slow down fish activity and they would survive without food. They will stay healthy, though obviously slimmer, after a week or so without food this way.

Culturing live foods for adult killies is next!

7.3 Food Self-Cultured For Adults

We will cover **daphnia, brine shrimp,** and **Grindal worm**. First of all, we need to order a starter culture.

The daphnia culture has just arrived! Long before their arrival, we have to get their foods and homes ready. Daphnia feed on and live in green water. As shown below on the right hand side of the photo, green water is full of green algae and its green is so thick that visibility is just about an inch or two. I was starting to prepare a second tank of green water on the left. You don't have to use fish tanks like I do. You can use any container that you have.

To prepare green water, use only aged water from your aquarium. Add some live plants, a leaf of your favourite vegetables like lettuce, and very roughly half a teaspoon of yeast per two gallon of water. For the one foot tank shown in the photo, half a teaspoon of yeast is good for a few days as food to the green algae. Give the green water extended lighting by either bringing the light closer to the water surface, or by letting the light on for longer hours. Some people leave the light on for 24 hours until the water looks green in colour. Finally, extend an air-line from your pump and use an air stone to provide just a touch of air in the tank. Wait until the whole tank of water is green before you order your daphnia starter culture.

After introducing your daphnia starter culture into the green water, they will feed on the algae and multiply. Feed the algae with yeast every 2-3 days and keep the bright light on for extended number of hours every day. If you stop feeding the algae with yeast and light, a tank of water that looks green and thick will become clear in just two to three days. All the algae would be consumed by the daphnia and it would be too late at this time to do anything to save the daphnia.

Daphnia need water change too. Since you are doing water change twice a week with your aquariums, you shall make a new container of green water, out of the water from your aquarium, twice a month. When the new container of green water is ready, net the daphnia to the new container.

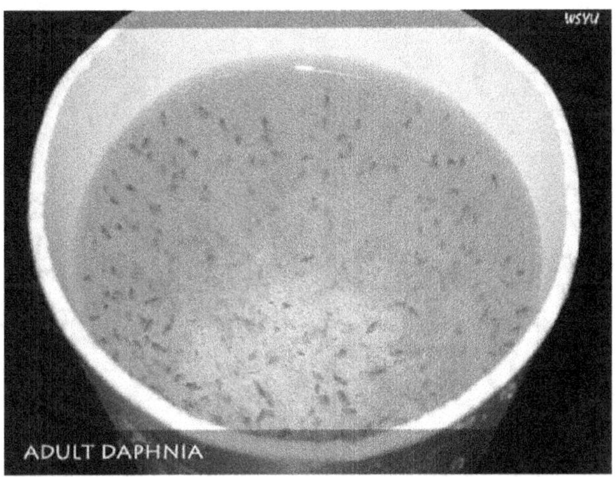

Before feeding them to the fish, I will put them in a cup of water. It is like a quick bath. The water is from the tap but I let it sit in the cup for at least 30 minutes to get rid of the chlorine. And of course, I keep several nets. Daphnia, baby brine shrimp, adult brine shrimp, and the fish all have their own nets.

Brine Shrimp - Adult brine shrimp could be raised from baby brine shrimp (see section 7.1) just like Daphnia. Try it and it is fun!

Grindal worm is in fact more popular than daphnia and other kinds of worm as they are not demanding on food and temperature. Some worms thrive only in cool temperature but Grindal worms still do very well in hotter weather. **Grindal worm are simply a lot easier to raise**. To start, we give them a moist bed of coconut fibre. Alternatively, you can replace coconut fibre with a piece of sponge.

Put coconut fibre in a small plastic box with lid, size about 4x6-inches to start with. Wet the fibre or sponge so that they are moist but not wet. You can now transfer your Grindal worm starter culture onto the top of fibre or sponge. Put a few grains of oats or cereal on top of the fibre and wet them with a few drops of water. Add only enough amount of food that the worms will eat in a single day. Experiment to find out how much that would actually be.

Before closing the lid, put a small piece of glass on top of the worms and food. Put the container away from direct lighting. Punch some fine holes for air to get in if the box is air-tight. As the culture develops, the worms come together around their food on the bottom of the sheet of glass. Be patient and wait until the starter culture quantity multiply by several folds before feeding some of them to your fish. To feed, simply take the piece of glass out and scrape the worms off. Just like culturing other live foods, you should prepare a second box of Grindal worm as a backup.

For daphnia, you know things are going wrong if the water start clearing up or that the number of daphnia is not multiplying. For Grindal worm, you know things are going wrong if the worms are not multiplying or trying to escape! If they start crawling on the side walls of your container, your bed of fibre or sponge is no longer good. Replace with new fibre.

End of Chapter Seven

NOTHOBRANCHIUS KILOMBEROENSIS MINEPA TAN 00-14

WSYV
FUNDULOPANCHAX GRESENSI TAKWAI

Chapter 8. Fish Photography

8.0 Introduction

The colour pattern that a fish exhibits is very much dependent on the quality, amount, and direction of light shining on the fish. Together with your choice of making the image brighter or darker using a combination of Shutter Speed, Aperture, and ISO settings of your camera, you decide what mood the image is to convey. That is the interesting part of fish photography. And that is the easy part.

The tough part is, you have to make sure that the fish is sharp or in focus in your image. To be able to do that, you need a camera that allows manual focusing and you need to spend one evening practising doing just that with that camera.

8.1 Colour and Lighting

Fish exhibit various colours under different lighting conditions. It is fun to try different setups to see which one is better for each particular species.

The colourful patterns of most Chromaphyosemion exhibited under strong flash light (right) would be all gone when put under normal aquarium lighting (left).

This species could look totally brown when a flash light is used at night (right).

Quite colourful when a flash light is used (right) but the look is rather unnatural.

No flash light was used in either case. The one on the left was under normal aquarium lighting while the one on the right was under subdued lighting at night.

Above: Top - Under normal aquarium lighting, the blue and orange colour of Blue Gularis is quite pronounced. Middle - If we use a flash light and set its output power to low, the blue will be gone while some orange remains. Bottom - If we set the output power of the flash light to high, the orange colour will be gone as well.

In some instances, for example, when the aquarium light was turned off at night and we try to catch what they are doing in the dark, using camera flash is the only option. Name of killies: **Chromaphyosemion LOE Makondo** (left) & **Chromaphyosemion Alpha Cap Santa Clara DNA 01** (right).

8.2 White Balance

Like fish colour, the overall image colour varies with the kind of lighting used. The White Balance (WB) of a camera when set to AUTO, the camera will try all it can to capture and display colours as close to what our eyes see as possible. If AUTO fails to produce the desired results, i.e. capturing and displaying white colour as white or very close to white, we need to try settings other than AUTO. Some common White Balance settings are fluorescent light, tungsten light, outdoor sunny, and outdoors cloudy, etc. Try all of them one by one to see which one works the best at that particular time, location, and lighting conditions.

8.3 Shutter Speed, Aperture, and ISO

Fish photography is too difficult for most consumer grade cameras to handle fully automatically. Aquarium fluorescent lighting is often too dim, the size of fish is too small, and the fish is almost always in motion. We have no choice but to learn taking photos manually.

There are three settings of a camera that we can use to control how bright an image is going to be captured. They are Shutter Speed, Aperture, and ISO. Lets start now with Shutter Speed.

Shutter Speed - Fish could be fast moving and if we instruct our camera to record too long a period of time of the fish, we could get blurred photos as follows.

Too Slow A Shutter (A Photoshop Emulation)

For example, 1/2 second is a longer exposure or a slower Shutter Speed than 1/30 second. When the exposure time is set long enough using a slow Shutter Speed and captured the fish in more than one position along its path in our image, we see **motion blur**, i.e. more than one image of the fish is shown one overlapping another. In the emulation above, two images of the fish were overlapped with a very minor offset. We can therefore see that the subject in the final image is unclear and that the fish has "moved".

To avoid motion blur, use a shorter exposure time or a faster Shutter Speed that captures only one instance of the fish in your image. As an example, if you found that a Shutter Speed setting of 1/15 second gives you motion blur, try immediately a faster 1/30 second and shoot again. If you still see motion blur, try a still faster Shutter Speed of   say 1/60 second and so on. The photo shown above is just about right.

In-camera or in-lens image stabilization of modern cameras or lenses will not help prevent motion blur. Such functions are good for stationary subjects only.

Aperture - Aperture controls the lens opening to allow more or less light reaching the sensor. Large Aperture is therefore good for dark shooting conditions while small Aperture is good for bright shooting conditions. Aperture is measured in terms of f/Stop values. The smaller the f/Stop number, the larger is the Aperture. To use a larger Aperture to let more light in, lower the f/Stop number either by turning the Aperture ring of your lens or by the pressing of a button at the back of the camera.

If we no longer see motion blur but the image captured is becoming too dark, we can try using a larger Aperture. For example, adjust Aperture from f/4.0 to f/2.5 will allow more light to reach the sensor and make the image brighter. In general, start your shooting session with a large Aperture or a small f/Stop number if you want to take control of this setting. Otherwise, **set the mode dial to S mode**. In S mode or Shutter Priority Mode, we select the shutter speed and the camera will automatically adjust the Aperture to give us the correct image brightness.

ISO - If the available light is dim, which is most likely the case with indoor aquarium lighting, the image may still be too dark no matter how large we or the camera set the Aperture. In this case, we have a choice of pushing the ISO setting up, for example from ISO 200 to 800 or more, to make the image brighter. In simplified terms, a higher ISO setting instructs the sensor and amplifier circuit to be more sensitive to light but in the same process, the sensor pick up more noise as well. Noise is mostly in the form of random grains and colour spots. Depending on the low light capability of your camera, you may be able to push the ISO rather high without seeing noticeable noise. When the noise get too noticeable in your photo, lower the ISO and use a flash light.

Higher ISO, say 800 or higher, instructs the sensor and amplifier circuit to magnify light signal more and therefore allows you to use a faster shutter speed and avoid motion blur. However, noise in the forms of random colour dots and dots of varying brightness levels will also be magnified and become noticeable.

Try using the lowest ISO value possible, say 400 or lower, to avoid noise and preserve the best details and colours.

SWALLOW GUPPY - SHORT MALE

Light flashed! The aquarium was dim and these guppies zigzagged way too fast. No matter how high an ISO and how large an aperture I set, I got motion blur. The image would be way too dark if I push the shutter speed faster still. In cases like this, use a flash light. Point the lens and flash light at an angle to the aquarium to avoid light reflection getting into your image. Clean the glass if you notice water marks or dirt on the glass surface.

A quick summary! Just read and move on!

ISO: A higher ISO value setting instruct the sensor to magnify the light it sees. Use the lowest possible ISO as the higher the ISO the more the noise.

Aperture: Open up the aperture by decreasing the f/Stop value setting will allow more light to reach the sensor. The more the aperture open up, the shallower the Depth of Field or area in focus. Depth of Field will be discussed in the next section.

Shutter Speed: A faster shutter speed means a shorter exposure time. To avoid motion blur, use as fast a shutter speed as possible but avoid making the overall image too dark.

Use a flash light if you still get motion blur after adjusting the ISO, Aperture, and Shutter Speed.

So when is an image too bright and when is it too dark?

Take this setup at night with aquarium lighting turned off as an example, the subject may look too dark if the shutter speed is set too fast. If we don't see motion blur, it would be fine to try switching to a slower shutter speed, say from 1/30 second to 1/15 second to make the image brighter. If we see motion blur, we have to use a faster shutter speed no matter how dark the image is. Since the subject is too dark and we cannot use a slower shutter speed, we open up the Aperture and crank up the ISO. Subject killie here: Nothobranchius-orthonotus-Nhangau-MT-03-4. It was 4-inch long. The SJO behind the plastic divider was 5-inch long.

The subject is now unfortunately too bright. So bright that some details on his head and body are blown out and lost. Lower the ISO,   use a faster shutter speed, or use a combination of both.

The exposure of the subject is now correct for the mood of this aquarium at night. Important details and colours are also preserved.

Rotate the image with our photo editing software so that the plastic divider is vertical in the image. Crop to finish.

In practise when taking fish photos, we could be very busy looking for good compositions and opportunities. We may therefore attempt to control only the most important setting - the Shutter Speed, for avoiding motion blur. We therefore will set ISO to AUTO and the mode dial to Shutter Priority or S Mode. In S Mode, we select the Shutter Speed and let the camera automatically adjust Aperture for optimal brightness.

S Mode selected.

The following is our section summary.

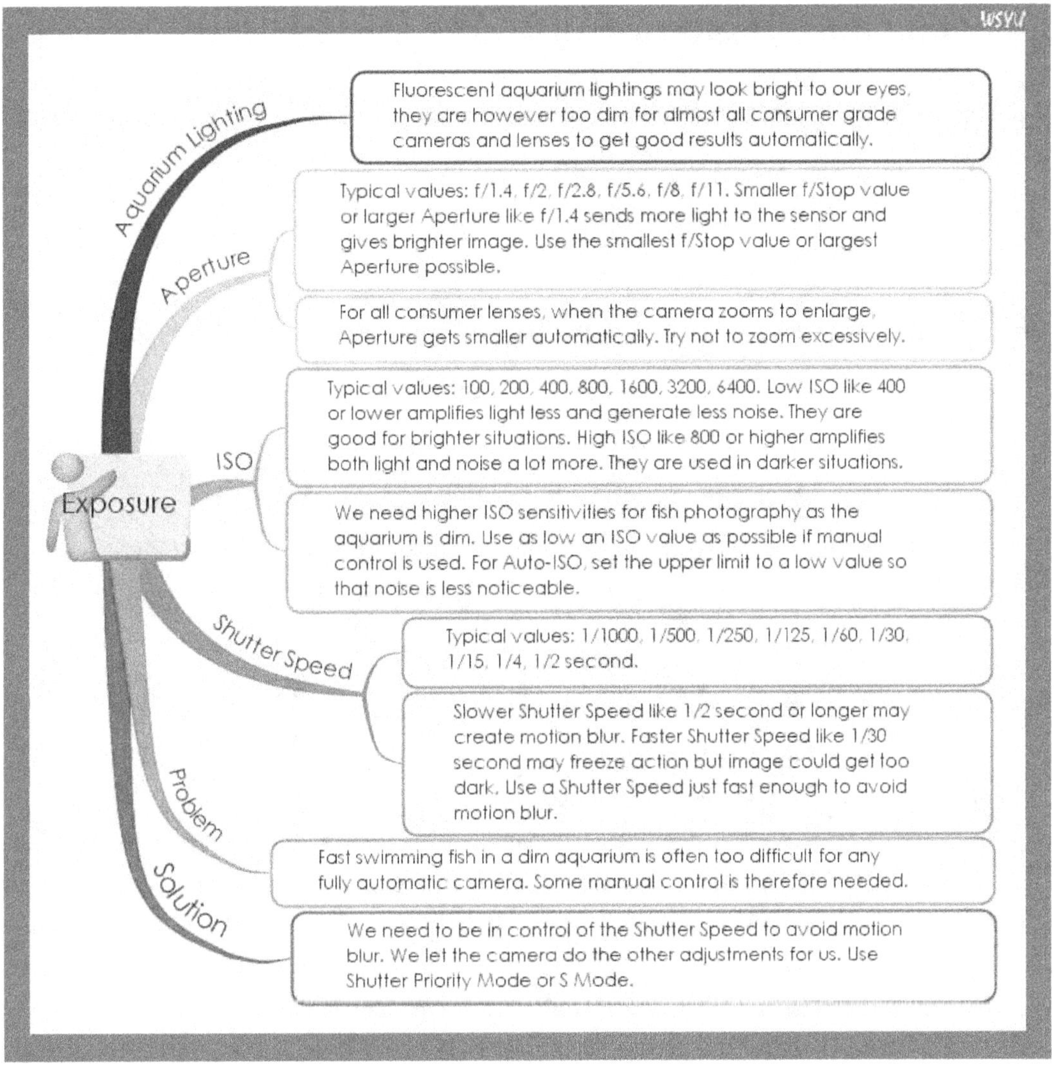

Exposure

Aquarium Lighting

Fluorescent aquarium lightings may look bright to our eyes, they are however too dim for almost all consumer grade cameras and lenses to get good results automatically.

Aperture

Typical values: f/1.4, f/2, f/2.8, f/5.6, f/8, f/11. Smaller f/Stop value or larger Aperture like f/1.4 sends more light to the sensor and gives brighter image. Use the smallest f/Stop value or largest Aperture possible.

For all consumer lenses, when the camera zooms to enlarge, Aperture gets smaller automatically. Try not to zoom excessively.

ISO

Typical values: 100, 200, 400, 800, 1600, 3200, 6400. Low ISO like 400 or lower amplifies light less and generate less noise. They are good for brighter situations. High ISO like 800 or higher amplifies both light and noise a lot more. They are used in darker situations.

We need higher ISO sensitivities for fish photography as the aquarium is dim. Use as low an ISO value as possible if manual control is used. For Auto-ISO, set the upper limit to a low value so that noise is less noticeable.

Shutter Speed

Typical values: 1/1000, 1/500, 1/250, 1/125, 1/60, 1/30, 1/15, 1/4, 1/2 second.

Slower Shutter Speed like 1/2 second or longer may create motion blur. Faster Shutter Speed like 1/30 second may freeze action but image could get too dark. Use a Shutter Speed just fast enough to avoid motion blur.

Problem

Fast swimming fish in a dim aquarium is often too difficult for any fully automatic camera. Some manual control is therefore needed.

Solution

We need to be in control of the Shutter Speed to avoid motion blur. We let the camera do the other adjustments for us. Use Shutter Priority Mode or S Mode.

8.4 Focus and Depth of Field

The fish is jumping out! Kind of 3D! Well yes, nonetheless the photo is bad. It is a pity that its head was not sharp nor clear while the rest of it was. This is not motion blur as we do not see multiple images of the subject overlapping one another. The front part of the fish was **out of focus**. (Name of the fish: **Chromaphyosemion bitaeniatum Ijebu Ode**.)

From the above photo, we can see that there is a **Depth of Field** (**DOF**) of at most a few inches deep outside of which every thing become unclear or out of focus. Even though a shallow Depth of Field helps to make the subject stand out by blurring the background, it makes capturing the whole subject in focus difficult.

Depth of Field or **DOF** is not a constant. It depends basically on four things:

Sensor Size: The larger the sensor the shallower the DOF.

Focal Length: Or how much you zoomed. The longer the focal length or the more you zoom, the shallower the DOF.

Aperture: The smaller the f/Stop value or the larger the Aperture, the shallower the DOF.

Distance from Camera to the Fish: Or the Focal Distance. The closer you stand the shallower the DOF.

If we take a photo of the aquarium by standing say 6-ft or 2-m away from the aquarium, a Depth of Field of say 2-ft or 0.7-m will make most of the aquarium and everything in it in focus. Unfortunately since the fish are small, we would stand right in front of the aquarium for taking their photos. For such a close distance to our subject, the Depth of Field is bound to be shallow no matter what camera and camera settings we use. Think of a Depth of Field of no more than 2-in or 5-cm deep when taking fish photos.

Depending on the photo composition, it might be fine or even great if only part of the fish is in focus. However, the part in focus is better be its eye, as shown above.

In addition to Depth of Field, please note that there is a **Minimum Focusing Distance** for each camera and lens combination. If we get closer to the subject than this distance, nothing will be in focus. So get close but never too close! Check the specifications of your camera or lens to learn about it.

It is now time to go take some pretty fish photos again!

An initial focusing is done **manually** so that at least part of the aquarium is in focus or sharp. Since we can tell from the display that the front part of the plant is sharp and in focus, we know that if we move our camera a little bit closer to the fish with our arms and press the shutter immediately again, the fish will be in focus.

Unfortunately in this case, we moved just a little bit too close. The fish behind is now sharp but the fish closer to us is not. We will quickly move our camera back just a touch and press the shutter again.

Both of our subjects are in focus! One more keeper to be admired by our fellow forum members!

The following is our section summary.

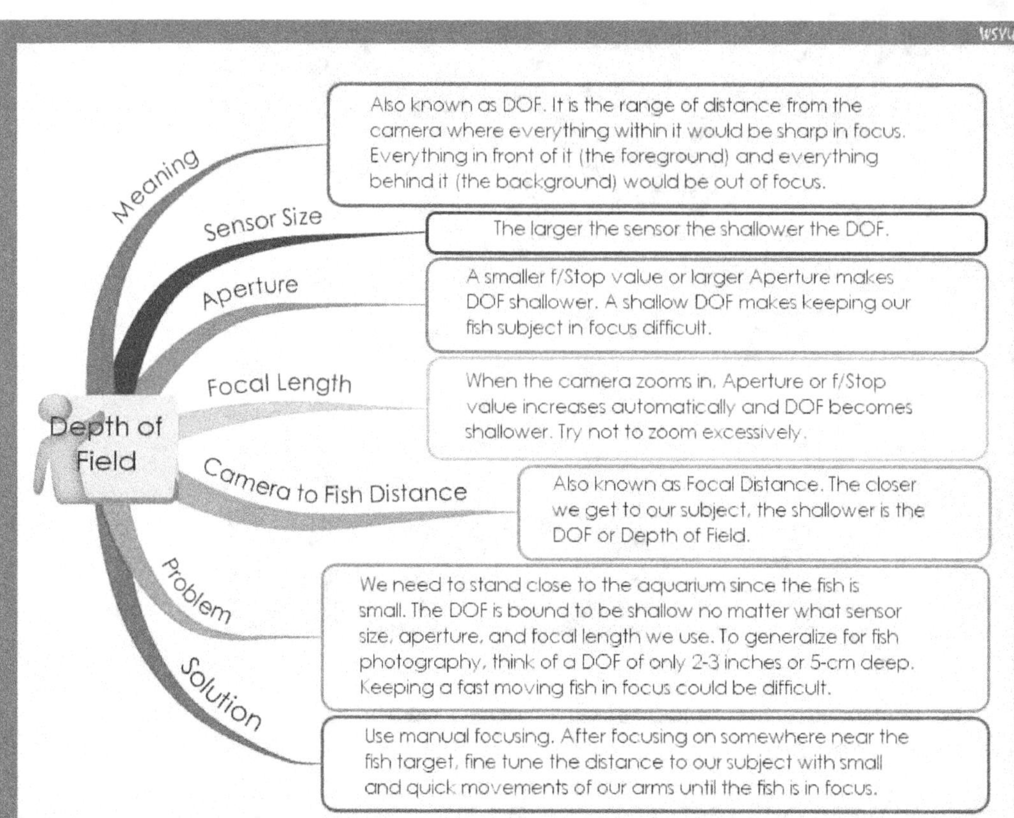
Meaning
Sensor Size
Aperture
Focal Length
Camera to Fish Distance
Problem
Solution
Depth of Field
Also known as DOF. It is the range of distance from the camera where everything within it would be sharp in focus. Everything in front of it (the foreground) and everything behind it (the background) would be out of focus.
The larger the sensor the shallower the DOF.
A smaller f/Stop value or larger Aperture makes DOF shallower. A shallow DOF makes keeping our fish subject in focus difficult.
When the camera zooms in, Aperture or f/Stop value increases automatically and DOF becomes shallower. Try not to zoom excessively.
Also known as Focal Distance. The closer we get to our subject, the shallower is the DOF or Depth of Field.
We need to stand close to the aquarium since the fish is small. The DOF is bound to be shallow no matter what sensor size, aperture, and focal length we use. To generalize for fish photography, think of a DOF of only 2-3 inches or 5-cm deep. Keeping a fast moving fish in focus could be difficult.
Use manual focusing. After focusing on somewhere near the fish target, fine tune the distance to our subject with small and quick movements of our arms until the fish is in focus.

8.5 Taking The Photos - Killies or Not

These are the steps taking fish photos.

1. Clean both the inside and outside of the aquarium if time permits.

2. If possible, turn all indoor light off except that of the aquarium. We want to minimize light reflection of the indoor lighting from the tank.

3. Even when all indoor lights are turned off, examine the display of the camera to ensure there is no unwanted light reflection from the aquarium, e.g. light from a window. Adjust the camera position and pointing angle until you don't see a reflection.

4. If a flash light is used, set the flash power low to start with. Point at an angle to the glass when shooting. Make the front end of your aquarium extra clean if you use a flash!

5. Set Mode Dial to S Mode. Set Shutter Speed to 1/30 second to start with.

6. Take a couple photos of the aquarium and check the colours. Is the overall image colour close to what we see? If not, adjust White Balance.

7. This is crucial. Use manual focusing. Auto focusing could be very difficult for a camera to achieve as the fish is rather small and that the Depth of Field is very shallow. Just remember to switch to manual focusing if automatic focusing fails. To manual focus, make an initial focus on the fish ore somewhere near the fish. To fine tune the distance to get the fish in sharp focus, move the camera quickly in or out with our arms.

8. If you see motion blur, try a faster Shutter Speed. If the image is getting too dark due to a faster Shutter Speed, crank up the ISO or use a flash light.

<u>Section 8.8</u> below describes an exercise that will make you a good fish photographer in just one evening.

8.6 Use of Photographic Tank

The majority of photos that I took were taken directly off the tanks where the killies live. But in cases when all I need to document is the fish itself, I use a photographic tank.

This much smaller tank, shown below, restricts fish movements within a very limited space and makes fish photography much easier. The most important thing to remember of course is to use water from the tank where the killies live. Other than that, try different setups as it is a big part of the fun.

Obviously, we can employ more than one model at a time!

Nothing around but empty space, he feels quite helpless.

Styrofoam (behind the tank) is not too bad.

I put the glass cover of the tank in to restrict his movement.

Or just put the tank on a chair with dotted fabric.

Obviously, they hate fish-net the most!

8.7 Other Shooting Tips

Try shooting from both left or right of the fish, especially when a flash light is used. Their scales are unidirectional and reflect light differently from different angles.

Try shooting from bottom up as well, as above.

At times, it is good to shoot something else together with our fish. To capture the more interesting top view of the yellow and red Cabomba above from the front of an aquarium, I took the Cabomba out of the water for half an hour and let it drooped due to a lack of lighting. I put it back in and hopefully, some fish would come by in front of the Cabomba before it stood straight up again.

Obviously, you don't have to shoot killies only! And depending on the colour and composition, sharpness is not always important, as above.

8.8 How To Advance Your Photographic Skills in One Evening

Practice makes perfect! You don't have to be perfect but you have to be good. You have to be good because fish are small and swim rather quickly. Most of all, they will not pose for you and we may not see them doing the same maneuver or display again. For this reason, if we have to practice 300 shots to be good, we should finish taking all these 300 practice shots in as short a time as possible or risk missing some really interesting shots.

The target skill to acquire here is to capture fish in good focus for at least 50% of the shots. 50% is an accomplishment and you know it if you have ever taken any fish photo before. For small fish targets like killies, auto-focus is quite often too slow. We need the ability to adjust focal distance manually and quickly.

We adjust focus manually in two general ways. Depending on your equipment, the first way is by either turning a focus ring on the lens or by pressing a button at the back of the camera body. The second way is by moving our arms closer or farther away. We will use the first way to make an initial focus setting and then use the second way of moving our arms to fine tune and capture the fish in focus.

When the fish is in focus or is just about to move into focus if we anticipate so, we need to press the shutter. If we don't, our subject could well be out of focus again due to the shallow Depth of Field. The key lies not in the quick movement of our arms or in our ability to anticipate fish movements. The key lies mainly in how fast we can tell that the fish is in focus by looking at the LCD display.

The one-evening exercise is as follows. Do not use a photographic tank for this exercise. Do not set ISO to AUTO and set the mode dial to M Mode or fully manual for the purpose of doing this exercise.

1. Take a photo of a fast swimming target fish. Press the shutter button fully when you think your subject is in or about to get in focus. There is no time limit in taking a photo.

2. Switch your camera to review mode. Take a good look at your photo for 10 seconds and 10 seconds only. Magnify the image if needed. Is your subject sharp? If not, is it motion blur or out of focus? What was wrong? What should be done differently? If you think you see motion blur and you want to try some adjustments, like a faster shutter speed setting, larger aperture, or higher ISO, go ahead and make the adjustment before taking another shot. If you see that something in the image is sharp and in focus but not the fish, how far is that sharp something behind of or in front of your fish target? That would be the distance that your arms should have moved for that shot. Stop thinking at the end of these 10 seconds even if you do not have an answer. Continue and shoot the next image.

3. Repeat step 1 & 2 exactly as described for 300 more times. Take breaks if you want but you must finish all 300 shots in one evening no matter how badly you think you are performing. (Well yes! If the photos are bad, it is your problem, not the camera's problem.)

The exercise may take only 2-3 hours or just about one evening to complete. At the end of the exercise, you would have acquired the important skill of telling what is and is not in focus from the LCD display without using magnification. Those in focus parts of your subject, e.g. its eye, will be shown in slightly higher contrast. Also, you would have developed a very good judgement of distance, and a very good grasp of how ISO, Aperture, and Shutter Speed affect your image exposure. In short, you will be a good photographer not only with fish, but with many other subject matters as well.

Since you have now become skilful in taking fish photography, the only things that you need to do is to be alert and have the camera around.

A fry holding something in its mouth is hard to come by. I quickly took my camera and pressed the shutter button. The fry was long gone before I could take a second shot! That fry was perhaps only 5-mm long and 1-mm thick. Getting it in focus in such a short time was really challenging.

Enlarged, that's a fry in its mouth! And look at the belly of the bigger fry! Life must be tough for fry when they try to hunt each other down!

8.9 Editing Photos

If you zoom too close and your subject is occupying too big an area in your composition or LCD, the chance of your fast moving fish getting off the frame or LCD will increase sharply. As a results, we zoom just enough and not too close. Cropping with a software is therefore often needed. Cropping will only be possible if your image is sharp and in focus, not because your sensor has a huge number of pixels.

I cropped two photos out of the above image. One is a close-up to show the species I keep and the other one shows the spacious environment they are living in.

After cropping, we may need to adjust the tone and contrast of the image to match what we see of the fish in real life as different made and model of cameras render colours differently. For the majority of cases, this may be accomplished most quickly with just an Auto-Tone command of a photo editing software. Automatic correction may not work well all the time and you may need fading the auto-tone effect using the software. Refer to your software user's manual for the steps to use. If you need a free photo editing software, download GIMP.

In the following example, I flashed since my aquarium light was turned off at night. The flash exposed every bit of dirt on the outside of my tank. I thought I wiped the tank clean before the shooting but I was not doing a good job. The following is the image before software editing.

Not bad to show what kind of environment he was living in! However, I needed a close-up image of him and so I cropped, as follows.

The dirt showing up as white specks became more pronounced and we have some touch-up to do. One way is to use Copy and Paste. Copy a position next to each speck and paste the copied content over the speck that we want to remove. Alternatively, your software may have a Healing Tool. With this tool, the white specks can be removed simply by clicking over them with the healing tool.

This is the touched up version with fish name added. Add a frame and watermark for copy right purposes if you need. Instructions of adding frames and watermarks should be available in the Help section of your software.

End of Chapter Eight

WSYU
FUNDULOPANCHAX SJOESTEDTI NIGER DELTA

WSYU
EPIPLATYS FASCIOLATUS ZIMIENSIS SL89

WSYU
APHYOSEMION PYROPHORE KOMONO YELLOW